Biblical Bits for Knit-wits

Knitting the Story of God's Love for You

Summer Mungle
&
Vicki Bedford

ISBN: 978-0615481210

Biblical Bits for Knit-Wits
Copyright © 2005, 2011
Summer Brooke Mungle & Vickie Bedford

Photographs by Vicki Bedford
Cover and logo design by *We Were Here Studios*
Book design by Summer Mungle and Vicki Bedford

Steps to Peace with God
by Billy Graham
Used by permission from Billy Graham Evangelistic Association, all rights reserved.

Unless otherwise noted, Scripture taken from the HOLY BIBLE, NEW INTERNATIONAL VERSION Copyright 1973, 1978, 1984 International Bible Society. Used by permission from Zondervan Bible Publishers.

For more information about the book, the authors, and the blanket, please visit:
www.biblicalbits.com

This book is dedicated to my mother:
my Spiritual mentor and lifelong friend.
Thank you for investing in my life and in the lives of so many.

Summer

This book is dedicated to the blessings in my life:

My husband, Danny,
My children:
Daniel
Summer
Sarah
My grandbabies:
Samantha, Jack, Callie,
and those to come…

I love you all,
Vicki – mom – nana

Knitting Explained

The patterns in the book were written with the beginning knitter in mind. Having taught knitting for several years I realized the difficulty knitting patterns present when they ask a novice to translate the language while they are still new to the craft! For this reason you will not see abbreviations as you would in a typical knitting pattern.

This book does not lay out explicit instructions of how to knit. For links to detailed video instructions, visit our website at: **www.biblicalbits.com**

Errata: Please visit our website before you begin knitting to ensure you have the most current version of the patterns. While you are there be sure to check out some unique ways to knit beyond the blanket!

Table of Contents

Introduction

Summer's Story

Knitting has become a part of my life, literally. My knitting goes most places that I do: airports, waiting rooms, restaurants, and the passenger's seat of the car. I meet many people from various walks of life who stop to watch, ask questions, and share stories.

Recently, my husband and I became house parents at a children's home in Georgia. Before I started my job, I knew what the girls and I would do our first week together. We would knit. Ken and I cared for up to eight children in the house, most of whom were teenage girls. They saw me knitting while watching movies or waiting with them at the doctor's office, and they asked if it was hard to do. When I told them that I could teach them, each one was willing to try. They were so focused as they picked out the perfect yarn, each with a specific reason for the color she chose. I learned something about each of the girls simply by listening to them converse in the yarn aisle!

That night, we gathered in a circle and I talked them through the basics of casting on and knitting. I demonstrated on my needles and they practiced on theirs. Each time one of them caught on, we cheered. As each girl learned, she went on to help someone else. By the end of the night everyone was knitting. Some girls were naturals, while others struggled. Their rows were not always straight, but they kept at it. I was so proud of them!

When a new girl came to the house the girls would say, "Miss Summer, we need to get her some knitting needles." Knitting became a way for us to get to know each other, share, and spend time together (most of it spent laughing at our mistakes). One of the girls said we needed a name for our group of knitters. After a bit of thought, I called out, "Knit-Wits!" They laughed, and from then on, that's what we were.

Four months later, at a staff Christmas party, I overheard a conversation. Heidi complimented Cindy on her baby's hat. Cindy replied, "I made it! The girls at the house taught me how." Cindy shared how our girls were knitting when she came over to visit, and they offered to teach her how to knit. I could not believe it! I was very proud of my Knit-Wits, and I thought about their actions the remainder of the day.

That night, God gave me the idea to share my faith using knitting. I thought about what happened: I taught a few girls how to knit, and they in turn shared it with others. What if we could share Christ while we knit? How many people would hear and share Him with someone else? I realized how similar sharing my faith was to teaching someone to knit; we explain the basics, set an example, and answer questions.

I began working on the idea for a book and shared my thoughts with my husband. He encouraged me to pursue it, and I continued working on the project. During Christmas, I shared the idea with the person I turn to for biblical advice, my mother. I asked her to write the devotional part of the book and she agreed. That night we stayed up until 4 AM sharing ideas. After taking pages of notes, we simmered them down to a devotional that pairs knitting with the Bible.

This book can be used in small groups or on an individual basis. If used in a group setting, I hope you not only grow in number but also in an understanding of how much God cares for you. Please do not turn away women who want to join your group after the first week. It is always the right time to share the Lord, whether it be the first week of your Knit-Wit Bible study or the last!

Each week a knitted square will be completed to serve as a visual reminder of the weekly lesson. At the end of the book, the squares will be sewn together to form a Story Blanket. This blanket will share the story of salvation and ways to grow in Christ.

When you complete this twelve-week course, I want you to walk away knowing how important you are to God and having a desire to serve Him. Please pray about starting a small group of Knit-Wits in your home or community. Take the book, your finished Story Blanket, and what you have learned and ask God to bless your ministry. My prayer is that people will find Christ, and share Him with others.

Vicki's Story

Whether I am teaching adults or babysitting children, I find myself telling stories. When Summer approached me with the idea of writing the devotionals for her knitting book, I immediately said, "Yes." The thought of being able to share Christ with others in such a unique way was exciting.

> *Likewise, teach the older women to be reverent in the way they live, not to be slanderers or addicted too much wine, but to teach what is good. Then they can train the younger women to love their husbands and*

children, to be self-controlled and pure, to be busy at home, to be kind, and to be subject to their husbands, so that no one will malign the word of God. (Titus 2:3-5)

I enjoy teaching. I have led the *Heart-to-Heart* Women's Bible study in Northern Michigan for the past ten years and I love it. We are a diverse group of women, with ages ranging from 13 to 82. We come from different churches but we share a common bond; Jesus Christ. We get together once a week to study Scripture, pray, and catch up with what is happening in each other's lives. We laugh together, and when someone is hurting, we cry together. By sharing past experiences, the women help one another. I think if God allows us to go through circumstances, both good and bad, He intends for us to share what we have learned with others. My prayer is that the stories and the questions in this book move you to become more like the women described in Titus.

God loves you, so much so that He gave His life to redeem you. You are precious to Him and He loves you just as you are. Satan wants us to believe that we are not good enough to be loved by God. We think we must clean ourselves up before we can approach Him, but the Bible says otherwise. God wants you to come to Him with all of your faults and all of your mistakes. He promises to cleanse you (John 13:4) and make you a child of the King!

> *You did not choose me, but I chose you… (John 15:16)*

I will never forget the look of terror on my friend's face as we lined the gym. The teacher picked two girls to be the captains; their job was to choose girls to be on the kickball teams. They chose the popular girls first, followed by those most athletic. Delores, neither popular nor athletic, was usually the last one chosen. Often I heard one of the captains say, "I guess I'll take Delores," knowing that she really had no option since Delores was the only one left to pick. Now, decades later I wonder...does Delores know that God chose her? Does she know that He thought about her before He created the Earth? Does she know that He loved her so much that He sent His Son to die for her? Does she know that His team will not be complete until she joins?

In the world's eyes, we may not be very important, but to God we are priceless. Listen, God is calling your name. He wants you on His team. How will you respond?

> *…**choose for yourselves this day whom you will serve**, whether the gods your forefathers served beyond the River, or the gods of the Amorites, in whose land you are living. **But as for me and my household, we will serve the LORD.** (Joshua 24:15)*

Materials Needed for the Lessons

- ❖ A Bible
- ❖ 340 yards of a medium or bulky weight yarn for the (MC) Main Color, 340 yards for the CC (Contrasting Color) and 340 yards for the border.
  - o We suggest *Vanna's Choice* yarn as a cost effective option.
  - o For the best variety of yarns, stop by your local yarn shop.
- ❖ Ruler or tape measure
- ❖ Size 9 knitting needles (see notes below)
- ❖ Row Counter
- ❖ Cable needle
- ❖ Yarn needle for sewing
- ❖ 1 yard of leftover yarn in colors: black, red, white, blue, green and gold (or yellow)
- ❖ Crochet hook to pick up dropped stitches
- ❖ Scissors

Choosing Yarn

1) Check the yarn label.
   a. Read the laundering instructions to ensure the fiber is washable.
   b. Locate the number of yards in the ball of yarn to determine how many "skeins" you will need.
      i. Hint: Choose colors that are opposite on the color wheel.
      ii. Avoid frilly, novelty yarns because they make it difficult to see the patterns form as you knit.

2) Needle size
   a. Check the yarn label for the suggested needle size.
   b. New knitters often knit tightly, so consider choosing a needle one or two sizzles larger than recommended.
      i. My favorite needles are wooden (bamboo or rosewood) because they are soft on the hands.
      ii. Metal needles are difficult for most beginners as well as those with arthritis.
      iii. Many new knitters find plastic needles a good choice because they are lightweight and sometimes help the stitches to stay on the needle.

We encourage you to visit our website at www.biblicalbits.com where you will find pictures of completed Story Blankets, links to websites with video instructions for stitches, and more.

The Story Blanket

To make the Story Blanket with a cross design knit 6 squares in the Main Color and 6 squares in a Contrasting Color, following the chart below. The finished size is approximately 30" x 38" once the 3" border is attached. This size serves well as a lap blanket or a baby blanket. Please visit our website www.biblicalbits.com for additional ideas and creative uses for the patterns.

Seed	Hidden in My Heart	Increase/ Decrease
Honeycomb	The Cross	Trinity
Stockinette	The Path	Garter
Stripes	Square	Basketweave

To create a blanket with a cross in the middle you must refer to this chart at the start of each pattern in order to determine which color yarn to use.

Designate a Main Color for the shaded squares (as seen above) and a Contrasting Color for the white squares of the chart.

The squares of the blanket can be made using one color or several and can be arranged in various patterns before they are sewn together.

Knit

I do not remember why, as an eleven year old, I wanted to learn how to knit. I don't remember any family members knitting; I don't think I even knew any knitters. I only knew that I wanted to hold those needles in my hands and create beautiful things. My mother must have been attentive to my desires because come Easter morning instead of the usual cellophane wrapped basket filled with jellybeans and hollow chocolate bunnies, I received a pair of knitting needles and a skein of yellow yarn. I held them in my hands not having the faintest idea what to do with them! There were a few instructions on the backside of the yarn wrapper, but nothing that I could understand. Sensing my frustration, my mother told me to go to our neighbor and ask if she could help.

Marlene said she had knit a few things years before and thought she remembered enough to get me started. That Easter Sunday, I learned the techniques of casting-on, knitting, and purling. I ran home determined to make a scarf. Sometimes the stitches were so tight it was impossible to slip in the needle to knit another row. I would slide them off and start over. Sometimes they were so loose that it looked strange and I would once again pull out the yarn and repeat the process. Over the next several days that skein of yarn was used and re-used so many times it began to unravel. I finally ended up with something that resembled a scarf.

Did you know that God is a knitter?

> *For You created my inmost being;*
> *You knit me together in my mother's womb.*
> *I praise You because I am fearfully and wonderfully made;*
> *Your works are wonderful,*
> *I know that full well. (Psalm 139:13-14)*

While I awaited the birth of my children, I tried to imagine what they would look like. What pattern was God using to make them? Was He using blue or brown for their eyes? Was He knitting with curly, blond hair or straight, brown hair?

When they were born and I held them in my arms, I thanked God for "perfect" babies. He did not use the same pattern when He knit them together so they are unique, one-of-a-kind creations.

With all the faults I have, it is difficult to believe, as it says in Psalm 139:14, that *I* am wonderfully made. As God knit me together in my mother's womb perhaps He dropped a few stitches! Sometimes I think I am knit together too tightly, other times I think my stitches are too loose, and at times I am sure my life is unraveling. However, God tells me that His works are wonderful. God loved me before I was born and He used the nine months I spent in my mother's womb knitting me together to be exactly who He wanted me to be.

> *For we are God's workmanship, created in Christ Jesus to do good works,*
> *which God prepared in advance for us to do.* (Ephesians 2:10)

The word "workmanship" actually means poem. I have also heard it referred to as "work of art." You are God's work of art! I have visited several museums and gazed with awe at paintings by some of the great Masters. Yet the best these artists can do is to replicate the work of God! Think about it. Their paintings are merely renderings of what God has created. We are the real poem, God's masterpiece. When He created the heavens, the earth, the plants, the trees, and the animals (Genesis 1:25), He said, "It is good." After He created Adam and Eve (Genesis 1:31), He said, "It is very good." The same Creator who made the universe and all that is within it, knit you together!

Men build beautiful museums and mansions to house the world's works of art. The Louvre holds Da Vinci's *Mona Lisa*. The Kunsthistorisches Museum in Vienna is home to several Rembrandt's, while St. Petersburg's Hermitage houses masterpieces by Monet, Cézanne, Van Gogh, and Matisse. How much more beautiful is the home God is preparing for us! He is creating heaven to house His "works of art."

Sometimes it is difficult to praise God for the way He made us. However, we can rest assured that He is the Master Craftsman and He does not make mistakes. We continue to fail in many areas, but just as the knitter must stop and figure out where she made the error, we too must consider where we are going wrong, repent and begin walking down the right path. When life gets hectic or I mess up more often than usual, I get discouraged and upset. It is then that I turn to the words of Peter and take his advice.

> *Cast all your anxiety on him because He cares for you.* (1 Peter 5:7)

The Greek verb for *cast* is *epiripsantes,* which means, "to throw upon." Imagine taking a fishing pole and casting a lure out into the water. It requires deliberate force. We are to take **all** our anxiety and throw it upon Jesus. However, unlike casting a lure, we should have no line attached with which to reel it back. He wants us to leave our anxiety with Him because He loves us. God's love and His forgiveness are infinite and nothing we have done or will do can cause that to change. (Romans 8:37-39)

I know that I did not create anything beautiful with that first skein of yarn and none of my knitting projects that followed were perfect, but that is ok. The joy, for me, comes with the sound of needles clicking together as the knitter moves the yarn up and over, creating beautiful things for those she loves.

1. Read Psalm 139:13-14. Can you praise God for the way you are made? If not, why?

2. Write the first four words of Genesis 1:1. What does it tell us about God?

3. Everything we see, we own, or we touch had a beginning. You and I were born; we had a mother and father. Someone built our houses. Someone planted the trees in our yard. Even the earth and the heavens had a beginning. How can we possibly understand someone without a beginning? Solomon was the wisest man ever to live and he had a difficult time grasping it too…

   I have seen the burden God has laid on men. He has made everything beautiful in its time. He has also set eternity in the hearts of men; yet they cannot fathom what God has done from beginning to end. (Ecclesiastes 3:10-11)

   When you think of God, what is the first thing you think of Him doing?

4. Now, add the fifth word to Genesis 1:1.

5. Try to imagine what God was doing before He created the heavens and the earth. What comes to mind?

6. Read Ephesians 1:4. God was thinking about **you** before He ever began to create this world. How does that make you feel? Explain.

7. How does it make you feel to know that He is **still** thinking about you and wants you to cast all your cares on Him?

8. What sins, cares, or anxieties are you carrying?

9. Why are you still carrying them?

10. Read Romans 8:38- 39. What can separate us from God's love?

*When you see the lock symbol take extra time to think about the questions. The answers will be the key to applying the lesson to your life.

Thought for the week:
There is nothing you can do to make God love you more, and there is nothing you can do to make Him love you less.

Pattern 1: Garter Stitch

When we create things with our hands, we spend time, focus our thoughts, and sometimes tap into a bit of creativity. We choose our yarn for a specific purpose: color, texture, elasticity, fiber content, or beauty. Just as we go through this decision making process when we knit, so God has done for us. He chose you! He has a factory full of fibers and He lovingly made each of us into a unique pattern. We cannot be replicated.

God, being our creator, knows every part of us, including the thoughts and feelings we strive to keep hidden. Let this be a comfort to you! We can share everything with Him! More than this; we can cast it all upon Him, knowing that He cares for us. As you "cast on" this first project, let your mind ponder the thought for the week and breathe a sigh of thankfulness.

Today's Pattern:

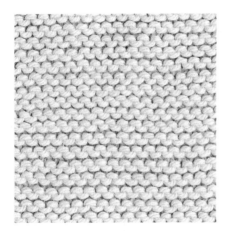 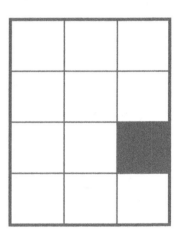

When you look at the finished square, both sides are the same. The pattern does not change, just as God's love for us does not change.

> *The LORD appeared to us in the past, saying:*
> *"I have loved you with an everlasting love;*
> *I have drawn you with loving-kindness." (Jeremiah 31:3)*

Directions:

Cast on 30 stitches.

Work in garter stitch (Knit every row) for 59 rows or until the desired length to form a square is reached.

Bind off and weave in the ends.

Place a safety pin near the corner where the cast on "tail" (the leftover yarn attached to the bottom row) lies. Later, this safety pin will assist you in the proper way to lay out all of your squares before piecing them together.

Weave in the loose ends of the square. To do this: thread your yarn needle with the "tail" of the cast on edge and weave it into the square. There isn't a set way to do this, but you should use your needle to move the yarn in different directions where it will be hidden. (Weaving in the loose ends prevents unraveling during laundering). Repeat this process with the bind-off tail and trim off the excess yarn.

Troubleshooting Tips:

❖ The garter stitch square tends to shrink in height after you bind off. For this reason, I prefer to knit until the length is almost an inch longer than the width.

❖ This pattern looks the same on both the front and back sides.

❖ When you start a row, wrap your yarn to the back in order to knit. Take care not to pull too tightly or your piece will begin form a triangular shape. On the other hand, if the yarn is wrapped loosely, your square will begin to grow outwards. The pull of the yarn is called "tension" and everyone's handling of the yarn is different. It may cause a bit of *tension* as you practice, but hang in there!

Personal Notes:

When it is time to bind off, I start at the opposite corner of the cast-on tail. Once finished, the tail from the "bind off" row will end on the same edge as the cast on tail. For each pattern in this book you can bind off in this manner. Having uniform squares like this make "seaming" easier when the time comes to stitch the blanket together.

If you need detailed instructions, see the links at: www.biblicalbits.com

Songs to knit by:	**Food for thought:**
Cares Chorus	Chinese noodles and chopsticks (looks
How Great Thou Art	like yarn and knitting needles)
You Knit Me Together	Shoelace licorice (looks like yarn)

Pearls

"Did you rub them on your teeth?" Paula asked.

"Did I what? Why on earth would I do that?" I responded.

"I heard that you can always tell if pearls are real by rubbing them on your teeth. Give them to me and let me try."

I handed my strand of pearls to her and watched as she ran them across her teeth. I am not sure that she knew what they were supposed to feel like, but I could tell from the look on her face that she thought they were real.

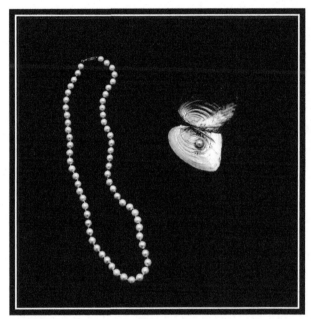

When Sarah, my youngest daughter, began first grade I felt the urge to join the world of women working outside the home. A new restaurant was opening up in a town about fifteen miles away and I just happened to know one of the owners. A good word from him, a five-minute interview, and they hired me as a waitress. I loved my job. I enjoyed talking to the people I waited on and I was thrilled when they rewarded me with generous tips. Most of my income went to buy extra things for our family but I put a small amount away every week. I had one goal in mind, to buy a pearl necklace. I remembered how classy Jackie Kennedy looked when she wore pearls and I wanted a touch of class in my own life. It took several months and a good sale at a local jewelry store before I could afford to buy my necklace. I loved how they felt against my skin and I loved how I felt when I wore them; a little bit classier and a little bit prettier.

Imagine, a little speck of dirt making me feel pretty! Isn't it strange how something as beautiful as a pearl starts out as an irritant? The oyster knows he cannot rid himself of it so he sets out to make it palatable. In the process, he produces a precious gem. Oh, that we would take the irritants in our lives and turn them into something beautiful. On the other hand, when we are irritating to others, it would be wonderful if they reacted by molding us into something beautiful.

Sarah loved my necklace. She would often sit next to me and touch the pearls. After a few years, the thrill of working outside the home wore off and I quit. I think that necklace is the only tangible evidence of my past employment. This past Christmas my husband and I bought Sarah a pearl necklace. When she wears them, I want her to know it is not the necklace that makes her beautiful. True beauty starts inside and shines forth for the world to see.

> *Your beauty should not come from outward adornment, such as braided hair and the wearing of gold jewelry and fine clothes. Instead, it should be that of your inner self, the unfading beauty of a gentle and quiet spirit, which is of great worth in God's sight. (1Peter 3:3-4)*

I am getting older and the "big 5-0" is just around the corner. Whatever beauty I had is rapidly receding into the crevices of my wrinkles. I pray that I will not let the world's idea of beauty become so all-consuming that I forget that true beauty begins within. Having a gentle and quiet spirit does not come easily to me, so I have to work on it continually by meditating on Scripture and praying. It is so much easier to dress nicely and trick the world into believing that I am a woman of worth, than it is to be pure and lovely on the inside. I am thankful that God will continue to mold me into the likeness of His Son, until I walk through the gates of heaven.

> *Being confident of this, that he who began a good work in you will carry it on to completion until the day of Christ Jesus. (Phil. 1:6)*

Sometimes I pick up my pearls and run them over my teeth. I understand that real pearls have slight imperfections that are felt by doing so. This reminds me that even life's most beautiful things are not perfect. I am so thankful that when God looks at me He does not see my flaws. He sees an imperfect woman, clothed in the righteousness of Jesus Christ.

1. How much time do you spend on your outer beauty versus inner beauty? (Hair, face, body, nails, clothing, and the time spent thinking about these things)

2. Is your beauty coming from the outside or from the inside? How so?

3. How is God using irritants in your life to mold or sharpen you?

   As iron sharpens iron, so one man sharpens another. (Proverbs 27:17)

4. Visualize a big iron rasp filing the edges off a large iron beam. The result is heat and friction. This action takes off the rough edges and makes it smooth. God said that we are going to interact with Christians in much the same way. Is it painful? Sometimes it is. Is it necessary? Yes. We need the friction to sharpen us and make us more like Jesus Christ. Sometimes, though, we use a big, coarse file when all we need is an emery board. Have you ever felt like another Christian has raked you over the coals when all you needed was gentle guidance? On the other hand, have you done the same to someone? Be gentle and make sure the motivation behind your actions is love. Write Philippians 4:5.

5. Are you willing to be molded into the likeness of Jesus? Even if it is painful?

6. Search the Gospels and make a list of the characteristics of Jesus. We cannot imitate what we do not know.

7. Compare the list from question 6 with your answer to question 2. What can you do to work on your inner beauty?

Thought for the week:
Beautiful things do not make beautiful people.

When knitting a project most patterns suggest you knit a square to check your gauge. The patterns in this book do not require you to check your gauge, but as you branch out in your knitting, you will most likely work a test swatch in stockinette stitch. This pattern uses the knit stitch and purl stitch.

Today's Pattern:

 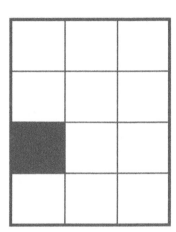

The back of the piece is full of irritants created by the purl stitch, which in turn produces a beautiful, smooth front. This reminds us to take the irritants in our lives and turn them into something beautiful.

Directions:
   Cast on 34 stitches
   Knit 2 rows
   Row 1: Knit to the end
   Row 2: Knit 2, Purl 30, Knit 2
   Repeat rows 1 and 2 until you have almost reached the desired length to make a square.
   Starting on the wrong side (purl side) knit 2 rows.
   Bind off and weave in the loose ends.
   Optional: place a safety pin in the corner as advised in Pattern 1.

Troubleshooting Tips:
   ❖ "Starting on the wrong side" means to begin knitting with the wrong side facing you.

   ❖ Beginning knitters often say, "I can't remember if I am supposed to knit this row or purl it." Here is a helpful way to remember just by looking at your work: The front is flat, so you will knit. The back is bumpy, think of these bumps as *pearls,* and *purl*!

   ❖ Consider making two more of these squares. They will be used with the upcoming chapters "Hidden in my Heart" and "Count your Blessings." (Remember to refer to the story blanket chart at the beginning of the book to determine which yarn color to use).

   ❖ When you finish the first few rows, you will see the bottom edge begin to curl. This is normal! The garter stitch border helps the piece to lie flat, as does "blocking" the finished piece, which we will address at the end of the book.

Songs to knit by:
Something Beautiful
In His Time
He Who Began a Good Work in You
How Beautiful

Food for thought:
Oyster Crackers
Tic-Tacs, white mints or gumballs
   served in oyster shells
Garbanzo bean salad

Baskets of Bread

When Jesus looked up and saw a great crowd coming toward him, he said to Philip, "Where shall we buy bread for these people to eat?" He asked this only to test him, for he already had in mind what he was going to do. Philip answered him, "Eight months' wages would not buy enough bread for each one to have a bite!" Another of his disciples, Andrew, Simon Peter's brother, spoke up, "Here is a boy with five small barley loaves and two small fish, but how far will they go among so many?" Jesus said, "Have the people sit down." There was plenty of grass in that place, and the men sat down, about five thousand of them. Jesus then took the loaves, gave thanks, and distributed to those who were seated as much as they wanted. He did the same with the fish. When they had all had enough to eat, he said to his disciples, "Gather the pieces that are left over. Let nothing be wasted." (John 6:5-12)

There were never leftovers when Eva made rolls. Whenever there was a potluck dinner at church, she brought homemade rolls. Eva was always smiling, always full of joy. Her eyes actually twinkled. If you didn't know her, you would think that she didn't have a care in the world, but those close to her knew differently. Eva lived on a fixed income but she never complained. She just trusted God to take care of all of her needs. No matter what she went through, her faith in God remained steadfast. Eva was a widow; her husband had passed away years before I met her. They had one child, a son named Billy. When Billy was in his teens, he was diagnosed with MS and eventually had to move into a nursing home. Eva drove there every day. When the MS progressed to the point where Billy could no longer speak, Eva just talked more. She read the Bible, told him stories, and talked about memories they shared. I have never seen a mother more devoted to her son.

Eva became a mentor to my friend Phyllis. Phyllis was a new Christian and was looking for someone to give her guidance in her Christian walk. Eva taught Phyllis lessons that she will carry with her the rest of her life. She showed her how to get up and face each day with a smile, how to love her children, how to find joy in the simple pleasures of life, and how to trust the Lord no matter what happens. Finally, she showed her how to make those fabulous rolls!

Eva loved to dance. So much so, that she asked our pastor to make a rather strange promise. She told him that when she went to heaven she would be dancing with Jesus and she wanted the pastor to rejoice with her, by dancing at her funeral. He agreed to do so. Eventually, Eva passed away. At the funeral service, with tears in his eyes, our pastor kept his promise to Eva. Billy passed away a few years later. I can just imagine them in heaven, laughing and dancing.

No more pain, no more tears, and a whole lot of laughter.

So they gathered them and filled twelve baskets with the pieces of the five barley loaves left over by those who had eaten. *(John 6:13)*

I have a handmade basket. I keep it beside my bed to hold my Bible and magazines. Usually the last thing I do before I shut my eyes is drop whatever I am reading into it. Buford made the basket for me. He is married to my mom's cousin, Janette and they live in the beautiful Smokey Mountains of North Carolina. We make it a point to see them when we go down to visit my grandma. Buford is blind; he lost his eyesight when he was in his early 40's. He used to be a logger but now he makes baskets; beautiful baskets, perfectly woven using only his memory and his sense of touch. This is something he learned to do after he lost his eyesight. He has never seen the things he has created with his hands.

…I am sending you to them to open their eyes and turn them from darkness to light, and from the power of Satan to God, so that they may receive forgiveness of sins and a place among those who are sanctified by faith in me. *(Acts 26:17-18)*

Buford was also spiritually blind. His family often prayed that his heart would be turned to the Lord. A few years ago, God answered that prayer and Buford received Jesus Christ as his personal Savior. This past summer we traveled to North Carolina to visit my grandma, Gertrude Tippett. What a joy it was, when we entered church, to see Buford sitting in the pew. After his conversion, the words of the hymn Amazing Grace took on a whole new meaning to Buford and to those who love him: "I once was lost, but now I'm found, was blind, but now I see."

1. How did Jesus test Philip's faith? (John 6:5-6)

2. In what ways may Eva's faith have been tested?

3. How has your faith been tested?

4. Buford placed his faith in himself until he came to a point in his life when his spiritual eyes were opened and he placed his faith in Christ. Have you ever experienced something negative that caused your spiritual eyes to open?

And my God will meet all your needs according to His glorious riches in Christ Jesus. (Philippians 4:19)

I think there were twelve baskets left over so people would realize that Christ is more than able meet our needs. He wants to bless us abundantly. Unfortunately, we often do not have the faith to believe that He can meet our basic needs, much less bless us abundantly. We trust in our own abilities more than God's promises.

Now to him who is able to do immeasurably more than all we ask or imagine, according to his power that is at work within us, to him be glory in the church and in Christ Jesus throughout all generations, for ever and ever! (Ephesians 3: 20-21)

5. Why did Jesus feed the people before He taught them?

What good is it, my brothers, if a man claims to have faith but has no deeds? Can such faith save him? Suppose a brother or sister is without clothes and daily food. If one of you says to him, "Go, I wish you well; keep warm and well fed," but does nothing about his physical needs, what good is it? (James 2:14-15)

6. Are there people in your community who have physical needs? How can you help? When will you help?

Then Jesus declared, "I am the bread of life. He who comes to me will never go hungry, and he who believes in me will never be thirsty." (John 6:35)

 7. Who, in your community, needs to know that Jesus is the bread of life?

8. Are you willing to tell them? When?

Thought for the week:
Make a batch of Eva's rolls. Put them in a basket and take them to someone who is both physically and spiritually hungry. Share the Bread of Life with them.

Eva's Rolls

Oct. 31, 1956
(As written by Eva)

Heat 2 cups of milk slowly until a film forms. Pour into a bowl. Add 1/2 cup shortening, 1/2 cup sugar and 2 level teaspoons salt. Stir until all dissolved. Let set until lukewarm. In a coffee cup filled half full of warm water, add 2 tablespoons of sugar, and two packages of Red Star Granulated yeast. Let foam up some, then pour it into lukewarm mixture and stir well. Start adding sifted bread flour (about 6 1/2 cups total) and one egg. After it gets too thick to work with a spoon, use hands to knead, adding enough flour until you can work nice, but just enough so it will not stick to your hands. Take it up in your hands, smack it, and work some more. Then grease bowl and put dough into it to rise once, punch down and let it rise again.

Then take half of the dough, roll it out 1/4 to 1/2 inch thick. Form into a circle on board. Cut it like a pie, into 1/4s, then 1/8's, then 1/16's. Put a pat of water on each center point, and start from the outside and roll into middle.

Have cookie sheets greased, turn each roll over in some of the grease, and lay them on the point. Place 12 on a cookie sheet, so when raised they will not touch.

Bake at 350 until brown. I start on the bottom rack, and then rise to the next rack when they begin to brown on bottom, and then set the other pan on the lower rack. When I take out the rolls from the top rack, I raise the rolls from the bottom to the top. Take out and butter the top.

If you start these about 6:30 in a.m., they can be done for dinner as they raise fast with two cakes of yeast. My stove has a window in the oven so you can see what they are doing as they are baking. Have plenty of butter on hand, or jam or Karo and you will find they soon disappear.

Vicki's note:
You can use two packs of dry yeast or two cakes of yeast. Either will work. These rolls take about 5 hours from start to finish.

Your Recipe

Use this space to write down the recipe for your favorite dish so you can share it with your group!

The basketweave stitch seems to generate the most interest from non-knitters. People are often surprised that it is not made of several pieces woven together, but knit in one piece. It is only when you grab hold and search it over that you see the way the pattern is formed.

Sometimes we cannot see how things are working together in our personal circumstances. Our faith may be tested, but when we draw close to God and seek Him, we develop perseverance and a deeper relationship with Him. Even when we do not understand, we can trust. "Through many dangers, toils, and snares," God will continue to provide for our present and future needs.

Today's Pattern:

 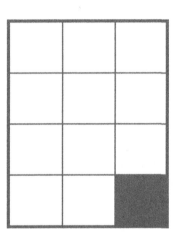

This pattern looks like the side of a basket. It reminds us of the baskets of food the disciples collected after Jesus fed the 5,000 and how God provides for our spiritual and physical needs.

Directions:

Cast on 34

Knit 3 Rows

Rows 1,3,5: Knit 2, (Knit 6, Purl 4) Repeat until 2 stitches remain and knit them.

Row 2 and 4: Knit 2, (Knit 4, Purl 6) Repeat until 2 stitches remain and knit them.

Row 6: Knit across the entire row.

Rows 7,9,11: Knit 2, (Purl 4, Knit 6) Repeat until 2 stitches remain and knit them.

Rows 8 and 10: Knit 2, (Purl 6, Knit 4) Repeat until 2 stitches remain and knit them.

Row 12: Knit

Repeat rows 1-12 until the desired length is almost reached.

Knit 2 Rows

Bind off and weave in the loose ends. *(Optional: place safety pin)*

Troubleshooting Tips:

❖ **The phrase "repeat," as used in Rows 1-5 and 7-11, means to repeat ONLY the directions in the parentheses**.

❖ Remember to use a row counter to keep track of where you are in the pattern.

❖ After you knit the entire row (on Rows 6 and 12) it is a reminder that the pattern is about to change.

❖ If you lose track or get behind on your row counter, look at your knitted piece, review what you have just knit and match it to the row in the pattern directions.

❖ I prefer to finish by working across Row 6 or 12, then knit 2 rows and bind off.

<u>Songs to Knit by:</u>	<u>Food to knit by:</u>
Amazing Grace	Eva's rolls
Great is Thy Faithfulness	Chex Mix cereal (resembles the basket weave pattern)

Count Your Blessings

I love antiques, especially antique quilts. When I look at them, I wonder who owned them. I like to think that mothers who wanted to keep their children warm at night made them. Some of the quilts must have taken months to complete. I own a quilt that is over one hundred years old and it has never been used. It is called a Bridal Quilt. A mother and daughter would spend months working on the quilt so it could be added to the daughter's' hope chest. Apparently, these were prized possessions even then. It makes me sad to think so much work went into something that was never used. It must have been stored away for decades. Perhaps she intended to pass it on to her daughter. Maybe she did. However, at some point, it ended up being sold to a stranger. I am that stranger and I too, store it away. If I used it, it would eventually get dirty and need to be washed. The thread is so fragile that it would not withstand a cleaning and I cannot bear the thought of it disintegrating.

Summer and I love going to auctions and estate sales. When we come home with our car packed with bargains, our husbands sometimes shake their heads and ask, "You paid how much for that?" Last summer we hit the sale of a lifetime. There were only a handful of people at the auction and only a few antiques dealers, which made it easier to get good deals. Summer has a passion for the 1940's. She hit the jackpot that day! Everything from clothing to furniture was purchased. Sometimes when the auctioneer yelled ,"Sold!" the purchase price was as low as one dollar. We laughed as we packed our bargains into the truck. In fact, the truck would not hold everything we bought! We had to drive 30 miles home and then make another trip to collect the rest of our purchases. Summer and Ken live almost 1,000 miles away, in Georgia. We are storing her "treasures" in our barn until they are able to transport them home.

Do not store up for yourselves treasures on earth, where moth and rust destroy, and where thieves break in and steal. But store up for yourselves treasures in heaven, where moth and rust do not destroy, and where thieves do not break in and steal. For where your treasure is, there your heart will be also. (Matthew 6:19-21)

As much as I love my "treasures," I love my family more. Our material possessions are not our biggest blessings, people are. None of my antiques will go to heaven with me but my prayer is that all of my family will be there. I am thankful that our children were saved when they were young, but we have other family members who have yet to trust in Christ. Because we never know how many days we have left on earth, we pray that they will turn to God before it is too late.

> *Show me, O LORD, my life's end*
> *and the number of my days;*
> *let me know how fleeting is my life. (Psalm 39:4)*

The weeks and years seem to go by more quickly the older I get. I have so many things I want to do but it seems like there are never enough hours in a day to accomplish everything. When I get up in the morning, I am already behind schedule. I struggle to find time to spend alone with God. I try to make it a priority, but at night, I often lay in bed realizing that I have failed Him once again. I repent and pray that He will show me how to use my time wisely. We need to be aware that our time on earth is limited and we need to stay focused on that which really matters: Jesus Christ.

> *Teach us to number our days aright,*
> *that we may gain a heart of wisdom. (Psalm 90:12)*

Notice that this verse begins with the words "teach us." If we desire wisdom, we must begin by asking God to teach us how to use our time appropriately. I recently received the following story in an email.

> Imagine . . .
> There is a bank that credits your account each morning with $86,400. It carries over no balance from day to day. Every evening it deletes whatever part of the balance you failed to use during the day.
>
> What would you do? Draw out ALL OF IT, of course!!!!
>
> Each of us has such a bank. Its name is TIME. Every morning, it credits you with 86,400 seconds. Every night it writes off, as lost, whatever of this you have failed to invest to good purpose. It carries over no balance. It allows no overdraft.
>
> Each day it opens a new account for you. Each night it burns the remains of the day. If you fail to use the day's deposits, the loss is yours.
>
> There is no going back. There is no drawing against the "tomorrow." You must live in the present on today's deposits. Invest it so as to get from it the utmost in health, happiness, and success!

Are you investing your time, money, and talents in earthly treasures or heavenly treasures? God tells us that we have work to do for Him here on earth. Are you ready to get to work?

> *Then Jesus came to them and said, "All authority in heaven and on earth has been given to me. Therefore go and make disciples of all nations, baptizing them in the name of the Father and of the Son and of the Holy Spirit, and teaching them to obey everything I have commanded you." (Matthew 28:18-20)*

Study Questions

1. List some of the things in your home that you treasure.

2. What do you think will happen to these things after you die?

3. What/who are your greatest blessings here on earth?

4. Are you using your time wisely? What needs to change?

5. You had 86,400 seconds today. How have you spent them so far? How will you spend the remainder of them?

Time spent	Time remaining

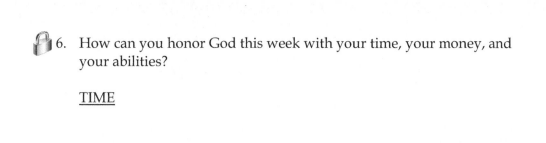 6. How can you honor God this week with your time, your money, and
your abilities?

TIME

MONEY

ABILITIES

Thought for the week:
My sister gave me a sweatshirt that said, "*The most precious things in life aren't
things!*" How true! Count your blessings and see how rich you are.

The finished result of today's pattern almost tricks the eye because of the depth created by knitting and purling. It reminds me of a piece of art; the longer you look at it, the more you notice. What do you see in today's pattern? At first glance you probably see a few rows of stripes, but there is something more! To see it, you must change your perspective. Lay the piece flat and look at it from afar or at angle. Do you see the squares?

Blessings are similar to this pattern. Sometimes our eyes are tricked by what we cannot see. We call these "blessings in disguise." Other times we look at situations and choose what we want to see. When I look at the pattern, I see four little boxes that remind me of presents. When you think of the blessings you have received, do you consider them gifts? Maybe you need to change your perspective to see how many gifts have been bestowed upon you!

Today's Pattern:

 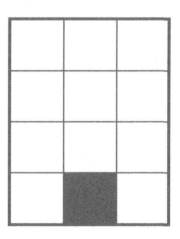

Look at the completed piece. It looks like a striped square, but what we don't see right away are four gifts hidden inside. Challenge yourself to "un-wrap" the situations in your life to see what blessings they hold.

Directions:

To Make the Background:

Make a stockinette square following Pattern 2: "Pearls," and set it aside.

To Make the "Blessings":

    Cast on 22 with MC

    Row 1: Using CC, Knit across all stitches.

    Row 2: Using CC, Purl 11, Knit 11

    Row 3: Using MC, Knit across all stitches.

    Row 4: Using MC, Knit 11, Purl 11

    Repeat Rows 1-4 three more times.

    Row 17: With CC, Knit across all stitches

    Row 18: With CC Knit 11, Purl 11 **the first time you work this row knit across all stitches instead.

    Row 19: With MC, Knit across all stitches

    Row 20: With MC Purl 11, Knit 11

    Repeat Rows 17-20 three more times, being sure to follow the directions carefully on Row 2.

Bind off and weave in the loose ends. *(Optional: place safety pin)*

Using a yarn needle and coordinating yarn, center the "presents" onto the stockinette stitch square and sew the two pieces together.

Troubleshooting Tips:

❖ MC refers to Main Color Yarn and CC stands for Contrasting Color.

❖ You will use two colors of yarn to make the "Blessings" square, but knitting with one color at a time. "Carry" the yarn loosely up the side of the square while it is not being used.

❖ Row 2 of the bottom section means: When working Row 2 you will NOT follow the directions as they are written; instead knit across all stitches using MC. After Row 2 is worked this way once, you will follow the directions as written each time thereafter.

Songs to knit by:	**Food for thought:**
Count Your Blessings	Petit Fours
How Could I Ask for More (Twila Paris)	Cake or any dessert cut into squares

Seeds

I live in a farming community; in fact, our house is surrounded by farmland. Last year our neighbor grew corn on his property. Long before the seeds are planted, the farmer spreads fertilizer; this is done even during the winter when they spread manure over the snow. In the spring, they begin tilling the soil and soon after, workers walk through the fields picking up rocks and putting them on trailers. They do not stop until the fields are clean. Now, mind you, we have lived here twenty-five years and every year they get  trailers full of rocks. I wonder if there will ever be a spring when they will not have to pick up rocks. Next, they plant the seeds. I am always amazed how those big tractors can make such straight rows. Soon I can see little green sprouts peeking out of the earth; a few weeks later the tractors make one last pass over the fields spraying weed killer, and by the end of the summer, the corn is over six feet tall and ready to be harvested. If the farmer had failed to do any of the preparatory procedures, the crop would not be so plentiful. Because the farmer is careful to do all the necessary steps, he is rewarded with a bountiful harvest.

"A farmer went out to sow his seed. As he was scattering the seed, some fell along the path; it was trampled on, and the birds of the air ate it up. Some fell on rock, and when it came up, the plants withered because they had no moisture. Other seed fell among thorns, which grew up with it and choked the plants. Still other seed fell on good soil. It came up and yielded a crop, a hundred times more than was sown."...His disciples asked him what this parable meant...

"This is the meaning of the parable: The seed is the word of God. Those along the path are the ones who hear, and then the devil comes and takes away the word from their hearts, so that they may not believe and be saved. Those on the rock are the ones who receive the word with joy when they hear it, but they have no root. They believe for a while, but in the time of testing they fall away. The seed that fell among thorns stands for those who hear, but as they go on their way they are choked by life's worries, riches and pleasures, and they do not mature. But the seed on good soil stands for those with a noble and good heart, who hear the word, retain it, and by persevering produce a crop." (Luke 8:5-15)

I suppose my grandma, Gertrude Tippett, planted the spiritual seed in my life. My earliest memories are of her singing hymns while she washed dishes. Others watered the seed. There was an elderly man who took my brother, my cousins, and me to church when I was in kindergarten. At the end of each service, we sang the song "When the Roll is Called Up Yonder, I'll Be There." I wasn't exactly sure what the words meant, but I knew that wherever "Up Yonder" was, I wanted to go there too. That summer another neighbor took us to Vacation Bible School. I don't remember much except that one day when she was driving, she took her hands off the steering wheel to show us how the power steering worked in her new, red car!

My parents took us to a Baptist church where every service ended with several people walking up to the front of the church while we stood, singing "Just As I Am." Once again, I wondered what the words meant and why people were up front kneeling down. Later, we moved and I went to Vacation Bible School with our new neighbors. It was at a Nazarene Church and I loved going. We had story time, craft time, song time, and at the end of the day we all gathered in the sanctuary for the closing. The director gave an invitation to come forward and accept Christ as our personal Savior. On Monday, Tuesday, Wednesday, and Thursday there was a spiritual battle going on inside of me. I sat knowing that I should go forward but I fought the urge until Friday. I sat in that pew through the final prayer, but could not sit any longer. The battle was over and Jesus won! Even though the invitation was closed, I still went forward. Two women took me to a pew and prayed with me. They were both crying. I could not figure out why they were sad when I felt so happy!

> *I planted the seed, Apollos watered it, but God made it grow. So neither he who plants nor he who waters is anything, but only God, who makes things grow. The man who plants and the man who waters have one purpose, and each will be rewarded according to his own labor. For we are God's fellow workers; you are God's field, God's building.*
> *(1 Corinthians 3:6-9)*

Christians are farmers. However, the seeds planted are spiritual seeds and the harvests reaped are souls. Sometimes we plant the seeds, sometimes we water them and other times we are there when the harvest is reaped. Being a farmer means a lot of hard work, many long days, and getting your hands dirty.

However, it is not without its rewards. One of the most thrilling opportunities for a Christian is to lead someone in prayer when they repent of their sins and give their heart to Jesus.

> *Do you not say, 'Four months more and then the harvest'? I tell you, open your eyes and look at the fields! They are ripe for harvest.*
> *(John 4:35)*

We are blessed to have Christians who teach us about Jesus, both with words and by the way they live. We often think of foreign countries as mission fields. Just look around. You live in a mission field. Won't you plant and water a few seeds today?

The Parable of the Seeds, Luke 8:5-9

1. Where did the first seed fall and what happened to it?

2. Where did the second seed fall and what happened to it?

3. Where did the third seed fall and what happened to it?

4. Where did the fourth seed fall and what happened to it?

The Meaning of the Parable, Luke 8:11-15

5. What is the seed?

6. What is the meaning of the first seed?

7. What is the meaning of the second seed?

8. What is the meaning of the third seed?

9. What is the meaning of the fourth seed?

10. Who planted and watered the seed in your life?

11. Who is the one who makes the seed grow (1 Cor. 3:6-9)?

Think of the people you know. Are there seeds that need planting? Are there seeds that need to be watered, or is there a harvest ready to reap? Are you willing to do it? One of the best ways to plant seeds is by sharing with others what God has done in your life.

12. Write down your testimony of salvation. If you have not trusted in Christ as your personal Savior, what is holding you back from being the fourth seed mentioned in Luke 8:15? If you would like to give your life to Christ, talk to the leader of your Knit-Wits group or flip to the back of the book and read "Steps to Peace with God."

Thought for the week:
Farmers know that without the **sun** there would never be a harvest. Christians know that without the **Son** there would never be a harvest.

Though many knitters complain while working on this stitch, it is one of my favorites. The motion of the yarn and needles makes you feel as if you are twiddling your thumbs. The pattern shows up quickly which brings about instant gratification, and the contrast of knitting and purling creates a texture that is hard to resist running you fingers across.

 As you knit *seeds* today, pray for the people who do not know Christ. They perhaps are twiddling their thumbs and biding their time. Others are looking for instant gratification in whatever seems right at the moment. Pray that they will find the One who gives us purpose and satisfies our every need.

Today's Pattern:

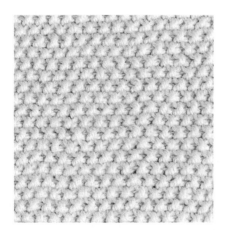 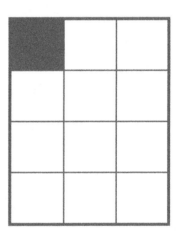

Look at your finished square; it is a field. Can you see the rows of seeds? Feel them. Some have just been planted, while others are ready to be harvested. Plant, water, and harvest the seeds in the mission field around you.

Directions:

Cast on 33

Knit 2 rows

Row 1: Knit 2, (Purl 1, Knit 1) Repeat until 2 stitches remain and knit them.

Repeat row 1 until the desired length is reached.

Knit 2 rows.

Bind off and weave in the loose ends. *(Optional: place safety pin)*

Troubleshooting Tips:

❖ The stitches should contrast at all times like a checkerboard. Think of the knitting as red and the purling as black.

❖ If you see a continuous line form, (such as in the stockinette pattern) it means you have made a mistake.

❖ Don't worry if you made a minor mistake- after all, not all seeds sprout!

❖ Remember, "**Repeat**" in Row 1 refers only to the directions in the parentheses.

Songs to knit by:

When the Roll is Called up Yonder

Just as I am

Prayin' Sowin' Reapin' (sung by
　Layton Howerton)

Go Light your World (Kathy Troccoli)

Food for thought:

Sunflower seeds

Pumpkin seeds

Poppy seed muffins

7 grain bread

The Path

"How much longer before we get there?"
"I'm tired!"
"I can't believe that we are doing this just to see some stupid tree!"
"Why didn't you let me stay at the campground?"

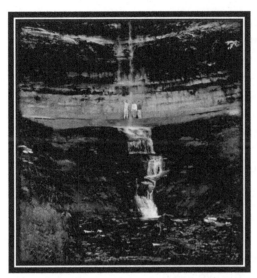

These are just some of the comments made while we were hiking down a path to see the largest tree in Michigan's Upper Peninsula. It was the summer of 1989 and we were on a twelve day camping vacation. I had thoroughly prepared for the trip by reading books on "must see sights." The previous day we hiked over one mile to see a beautiful waterfall and no one complained about that. They even enjoyed walking behind it and feeling the cool spray of water on their faces. I expected them to be just as excited to make the one-mile journey into the woods to see the tree. I have to admit that this hike was more difficult. The path was not clearly marked and we only met a few other people making the trek. Did I mention that it was 90 degrees outside and hiking in the woods was like being in a sauna? However, when we found the tree I was certain that it would be worth all the effort it took to get there. According to the crude map, the tree should have been within eyesight. We paused and looked around. I could not see the tree yet, but, as I told my family, it could not be too much farther.

"Ooooh, I can't wait!" This time the snide remark came from my husband. It was that remark that pushed me over the edge.
"That's it! I've had enough! Let's go back!" I yelled.

Knowing they were facing my wrath, all of a sudden everyone wanted to forge ahead. But, for me it was over; the excitement gone. I turned and headed back for the car, grumbling all the way. We followed quite a few paths that vacation and all but that one led to some place nice.

> *Enter through the narrow gate. For wide is the gate and broad is the road that leads to destruction, and many enter through it. But small is the gate and narrow the road that leads to life, and only a few find it. (Matthew 7:13-14)*

Last year my daughter Summer and her husband Ken bought a GPS (navigation system) for their car. She and I used it on our shopping adventure the day after Thanksgiving. They had only lived in Georgia a short time and she was unsure how to get to some of the stores. She typed in our destination and from that point on navigating was a breeze. The GPS told us when to turn, how much further to go, and when to turn around if we missed our turn. Wouldn't it be wonderful if we had a GPS for life's journeys?

Sometimes staying on the road God sets before us is exciting and many times, challenging. However, often we are just like kids, whining and complaining about where the path leads. We tell God we are too tired to go on and wonder when we will finally "get there."

Elijah was my hero when I was a child. I loved reading the stories of God sending ravens with food for him to eat (1 Kings 17:6), of raising a little boy from the dead (1 Kings 17:19-22), and especially about him challenging the prophets of Baal on Mount Carmel and praying for fire to come down from heaven. I cheered when God answered his prayer and sent the fire down to consume the sacrifice, the altar, and the water surrounding it (1 Kings 18). Elijah followed the path God set before him and God used him to do many awesome things. Then I read this about my hero:

> *Elijah was afraid and ran for his life. When he came to Beersheba in Judah, he left his servant there, while he himself went a day's journey into the desert. He came to a broom tree, sat down under it and prayed that he might die. "I have had enough, LORD," he said. "Take my life; I am no better than my ancestors." Then he lay down under the tree and fell asleep. (1 Kings 19:3-5)*

In many ways, we are like Elijah. God protected him through some of life's most difficult journeys, then for whatever reason, a discouraged Elijah ran away. Sometimes we venture off the path and take our own road. We get frustrated and quit moving forward. We sit and wallow in self-pity, making it difficult to hear the voice of God.

> *Then a great and powerful wind tore the mountains apart and shattered the rocks before the LORD, but the LORD was not in the wind. After the wind there was an earthquake, but the LORD was not in the earthquake. After the earthquake came a fire, but the LORD was not in the fire. And after the fire came a gentle whisper. When Elijah heard it, he pulled his cloak over his face and went out and stood at the mouth of the cave. Then a voice said to him, "What are you doing here, Elijah?" He replied, "I have been very zealous for the LORD God Almighty. The Israelites have rejected your covenant, broken down your altars, and put your prophets to death with the sword. I am the only one left, and now they are trying to kill me too." The LORD said to him, "Go back the way you came." (1 Kings 19:11-15)*

God *is* like a GPS! He does tell us where we should go and what we should do. Often we are like Elijah; looking for the voice of God to be loud and powerful. We need to be aware that the voice of God, as powerful as it is, sometimes comes in a whisper. We long to hear from God, but we don't want Him to say "turn around and go back into the difficult situation from which you ran." But then again, he never said that the path would be easy.

> *I have told you these things, so that in me you may have peace. In this world you will have trouble. But take heart! I have overcome the world. (John 16:33)*

Wait a minute! Is He saying that we should expect both peace and trouble? We want the peace without the trouble. Why does it seem like we have more trouble than peace in our lives? Perhaps we fail to recognize God's peace. It is not a matter of Him calming *the storms* in our lives but of Him calming *us* in the midst of the storms. Remember Peter (Matthew 14:25-31) walking on the stormy sea? He succeeded until he took his eyes off Jesus. When he did, he sank. I am no different from Peter! As long as I stay focused on God, my steps are surefooted. When I realize how big the storm is, I begin to sink. How wonderful that He is always ready to pull me out of the pit when I, like Peter, cry out, "Lord, save me!"

Staying on God's path is not always easy and not always fun, but always the right thing to do. Because of my anger, we turned back on that hiking path and never saw that incredible tree. We must stay focused on the path He set before us, because at the end we will see Jesus.

Study Questions

1. Have you ever been lost? Who found you or how did you find your way?

2. The Bible says the path to destruction is wide (Matthew 7:13-14). Why would you choose to follow the wide path instead of the narrow path?

3. When you travel on God's path, you should not take baggage. What baggage from your past are you trying to carry with you?

4. Are you ready to drop the baggage? If not, what is holding you back?

5. Has your anger ever interfered with your Christian walk? How so?

6. Like Elijah, have you ever been so discouraged with your life that you wanted to quit? What kept you going, or would have kept you going?

7. Have you ever felt like you were the only one trying to do the right thing?

During these times, God has not abandoned you. You need to be still and listen for His voice.

8. When have you experienced peace in the midst of a storm?

9. While traveling on the road to Damascus, Paul met Jesus, and suddenly his travel itinerary changed (Acts 9). When have you received directions from God concerning where to go or what to do?

10. Are you on the right path now or have you ventured off?

Thought for the week:
It is time we quit telling God how big our problems are, and start telling our problems how big our God is!

While glancing through today's pattern you will notice many rows of directions! They are not difficult, but require you to refer to the pattern frequently. A row counter will be helpful; think of it as a knitter's GPS. After 25 rows, you (like Elijah,) will head back from where you came, by repeating the rows in a descending fashion.

Just as the knitter refers back to her pattern to stay on course, so the Christian must constantly look to the Bible. Keeping our eyes fixed upon the Savior keeps us walking towards Him ready to accomplish whatever He asks of us. Sometimes while walking on the path, we get comfortable; our lives become a pattern of daily schedules with a "to-do" list that lacks God's desires, and instead reflects our own. At some point our path turns and God allows circumstances to change our direction without warning. When everything else is out of control, He is the constant in our lives. As you work on today's pattern, you will be reminded of this every time you see Knit 7 or Purl 7. They are the center stitches-exactly where He needs to be in our lives.

Today's Pattern:

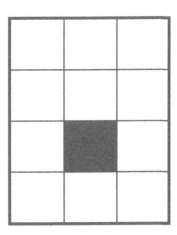

Look at your finished square. Notice the path feels smooth until you venture off and it gets bumpy. Although your personal path turns, live in confidence, knowing that He has purposed your steps; now walk them in obedience to His Word.

Today's pattern introduces a new technique: Knitting through the back loops. It is abbreviated as "tbl" in the pattern. This technique is optional- if it is too difficult, simply knit these stitches instead. The background is the difference between "knitting" and "knitting through the back loops." Choose the technique you are comfortable with.

Directions:

Cast on 34

Knit 3 Rows.

Row 1: Knit 2, Knit 16tbl, Purl 7, Knit 7tbl, Knit 2
Row 2: Knit 2, Purl 8, Knit 7, Purl 15, Knit 2
Row 3: Knit 2, Knit 15tbl, Purl 7, Knit 8tbl, Knit 2
Row 4: Knit 2, Purl 9, Knit 7, Purl 14, Knit 2
Row 5: Knit 2, Knit 14tbl, Purl 7, Knit 9tbl, Knit 2
Row 6: Knit 2, Purl 11, Knit 7, Purl 12, Knit 2
Row 7: Knit 2, Knit 12tbl, Purl 7, Knit11tbl, Knit 2
Row 8: Knit 2, Purl 12, Knit 7, Purl 11, Knit 2
Row 9: Knit 2, Knit 11tbl, Purl 7, Knit 12tbl, Knit 2
Row 10: Knit 2, Purl 12, Knit 7, Purl 11, Knit 2
Row 11: Knit 2, Knit 10tbl, Purl 7, Knit 13tbl, Knit 2
Row 12: Knit 2, Purl 13, Knit 7, Purl 10, Knit 2
Row 13: Knit 2, Knit 10tbl, Purl 7, Knit 13tbl, Knit 2
Row 14: Knit 2, Purl 12, Knit 7, Purl 11, Knit 2
Row 15: Knit 2, Knit 11tbl, Purl 7, Knit 12tbl, Knit 2
Row 16: Knit 2, Purl 11, Knit 7, Purl 12, Knit 2
Row 17: Knit 2, Knit 12tbl, Purl 7, Knit 11tbl, Knit 2
Row 18: Knit 2, Purl 10, Knit 7, Purl 13, Knit 2
Row 19: Knit 2, Knit 14tbl, Purl 7, Knit 9tbl, Knit 2
Row 20: Knit 2, Purl 9, Knit 7, Purl 14, Knit 2
Row 21: Knit 2, Knit 15tbl, Purl 7, Knit 8tbl, Knit 2
Row 22: Knit 2, Purl 8, Knit 7, Purl 15, Knit 2
Row 23: Knit 2, Knit 14tbl, Purl 7, Knit 9tbl, Knit 2
Row 24: Knit 2, Purl 9, Knit 7, Purl 14, Knit 2
Row 25: Knit 2, Knit 13tbl, Purl 7, Knit 10tbl, Knit 2

*Now, you will repeat rows. Start on Row 18 and work towards the top
(Row 17, 16, 15, continuing until you have almost reached the desired length)
Knit 3 rows
Bind off and weave in the loose ends. *(Optional: place safety pin)*

Troubleshooting Tips:

❖ If you do not have a row counter, use a pencil to mark off the rows as you complete them.

❖ Before you bind off, the instructions say, "Knit 3 rows." I prefer to start this section with the wrong side facing me.

Songs to knit by:	Food for thought:
Thy Word: Amy Grant	Rocky Road Ice Cream
Walk by Faith: Jeremy Camp	Trail Mix
Steady On: Point of Grace	Chocolate Candy Rocks

Increase/Decrease

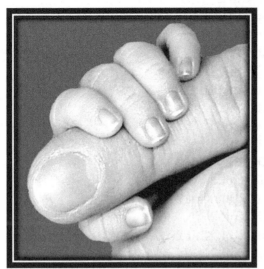

On Mother's Day in 2001, our friends, Art and Terry, were informed that a young woman chose them to be the parents of her unborn baby. Only months before, another young women made the same choice. In January, they came home from the hospital with a beautiful little girl. Later Art and Terry were devastated when the birth mother changed her mind and took her child back. Despite their grief, they continued to trust that God would give them the desire of their heart: a baby. For that reason, we were elated to get the news that a son or daughter would soon be theirs. We prayed that all would go well this time.

One day my mother-in-law and I were talking and I told her that she gave me the best present I had ever received.

She paused, and said, "What did I ever give to you that was so good?"
"You took a little boy and raised him to be a wonderful man. Then you gave him to me to be my husband. Danny is the best gift I ever received." I replied.

She chuckled a little and said, "Ah, I didn't do anything special." It was just like Margaret to say that, as she was a meek, humble woman.

Not too long after that conversation, we stood by her hospital bed. Margaret had surgery to repair a broken hip and shortly thereafter she developed pneumonia. The doctors did what they could and then left her in the hands of God. As we waited for the inevitable, Art and Terry stopped by. They were at the hospital not only to comfort us, but also to witness the birth of their child. You see, just down the hall, the birth mother was in labor. The size of the Bedford family was going to decrease and the Ross family would increase.

Duncan Morrison Ross was born at 12:45 P.M. and Margaret passed minutes later. We left her hospital room, walked down a hallway and into another hospital room to hold Duncan. I felt the clasp of one hand go limp only to feel the grasp of a newborn baby. It seemed almost surreal, walking from death to new life.

I tell you the truth, whoever hears my word and believes him who sent me has eternal life and will not be condemned; he has crossed over from death to life. (John 5:24)

When we trust in Christ as our Savior, we pass from death to life, marking the beginning of the journey. The faithful men and women in Scripture offer us opportunities to learn more about the Lord by examining their actions. One lesson I learned was from John the Baptist.

Of everything John said, I think John 3:30 states one of the most challenging.

He must increase; I must decrease. (John 3:30)

John said he was not worthy to untie the laces on Jesus' sandals, but went on to say he had to become less, so Jesus would become greater. The act of taking off shoes and washing guest's feet was a job belonging to the lowest slave. I think John was saying he needed to be lower than the lowest slave.

It cannot be denied that John had some very strange ways, eating locusts and wearing clothes made of camel's hair (Matthew 3:4), but Jesus had this to say about him.

I tell you, among those born of women there is no one greater than John. (Luke 7:28)

Intrigued by this verse, I started studying the life of John the Baptist. Along with the things I already mentioned, I also learned:

❖ He was named by God (Luke 1:13).
❖ He was filled with the Holy Spirit before birth (Luke 1:15).
❖ He was great in the eyes of the Lord (John 1:15).
❖ He was a joy and a delight to his parents (Luke 1:14).
❖ He did not drink wine or other fermented drink (Luke 1:15).
❖ He prepared the way for the Lord (Malachi 3:1).
❖ He brought many Israelites, who had fallen away, back to the Lord (Luke 1:16).
❖ He had the power and spirit of Elijah (Luke 1:17).
❖ He turned the hearts of fathers to their children, as well as the disobedient to the wisdom of the righteous (Luke 1:17).
❖ He was filled with joy at the sound of Jesus' voice (John 3:29).
❖ He called for people to be prepared to meet the Lord (Isaiah 40:3, Luke 1:17, John 1:23).
❖ He baptized people (John 1:28).
❖ He recognized that Jesus would pay the penalty for our sins (John 1:29).
❖ He preached repentance (Matthew 3:1, Mark 1:15).
❖ He was not afraid of "religious leaders" (Matthew 3:7).
❖ He recognized his own need for baptism by Christ (Matthew 3:13).

- ❖ He was obedient (Matthew 3:15).
- ❖ He discipled people (Matthew 11:7).
- ❖ He was a prophet (Matthew 11:9).
- ❖ He was a light in the darkness (John 5:35).
- ❖ He predicted that Jesus would baptize with the Holy Spirit and with fire (Matthew 3:11), which happened on Pentecost.
- ❖ He called Jesus "the Son of God" (John 1:34).
- ❖ He was humble (John 1:27).
- ❖ He was hated and some wanted him dead (Mark 6:19).
- ❖ He was imprisoned for confronting the king's sexual sin (Matthew 14:3-4).
- ❖ He was beheaded (Matthew 14:10).
- ❖ His death caused Jesus to withdraw from everyone (Matthew 14:13).

Wow! What a lesson in humility. I am not thrilled at the thought of doing "lowly" jobs. I do not like to admit when I am wrong and I do not like when someone else gets credit for work that I do. As you may have figured out, I struggle with pride. When I examine myself, I realize there is far too much "me" and far too little "Jesus" in my life. John was correct, I must decrease and He must increase.

1. Based on what you know about John the Baptist, how are you most like him?

2. Which areas of your life do you wish resembled his?

3. What areas in your life need "decreasing"?

4. Do others think of you as a humble person?

5. Read Proverbs 13:10, 16:18-19, 29:23 and Isaiah 13:10. What does God say about pride?

6. If Christ is to increase in our lives, we must rid ourselves of all pride. In what areas of your life does pride exist?

For by the grace given me I say to every one of you: Do not think of yourself more highly than you ought, but rather think of yourself with sober judgment, in accordance with the measure of faith God has given you. (Romans 12:3)

7. Write a letter to God telling Him about your struggles and ask Him to help you overcome them.

Thought for the week:
If a spiritual mirror were held before you, would it reflect your image or the image of Jesus Christ?

The pattern today includes two new techniques: increasing and decreasing. There are a few different ways to accomplish these tasks. We will be using "yarn over" to increase and "knit 2 together" to decrease. When done correctly, a pretty eyelet pattern forms.

In knitting, decreasing is a matter of taking out what does not belong. Without taking away then giving back, the pattern will not form. The same is true for you; unless you allow God to take away "self" and replace it with "Jesus", you stand in the way of all that His pattern for your life offers.

Today's Pattern:

 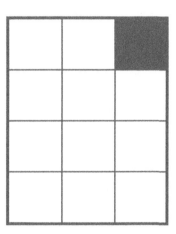

Hold the piece up to the sun. Can you see light shining through? We must "decrease" so that Christ (the Son) shines through in our lives.

Directions:

Cast on 34

Knit 2 rows

Row 1: Knit across the row.

Row 2: Knit 2, Purl 30, Knit 2

Row 3: Knit 2, (Knit 2, Knit 2 together, Yarn Over) Repeat what is in the parentheses until 4 stitches remain and knit them.

Row 4: Knit 2, Purl 30, Knit 2

Row 5: Knit across the row.

Row 6: Knit 2, Purl 30, Knit 2

Row 7: Knit 2, (Knit 2 together, Yarn Over, Knit 2) Repeat until 4 stitches remain and Knit 2 together, Yarn Over, Knit 2

Row 8: Knit 2, Purl 30, Knit 2

Repeat Rows 1-8 four more times or until the desired length is reached.

Knit 2 rows starting on the wrong side (the back).

Bind off and weave in the loose ends. *(Optional: place safety pin)*

Troubleshooting Tips:

❖ A pattern of staggered eyelets (holes) will begin to form. Look for the eyelets to form diagonally.

❖ Remember to maintain the tension of your yarn throughout the entire piece.

❖ I prefer to finish on Row 1 or Row 5, knit 2 rows and bind off.

Songs to knit by:	Food for thought:
In the Middle of Me	Large / miniature candy bars
You Say If I will Come and Pray to You (by Rebecca St James)	Large / mini Oreo cookies
	Ritz / mini Ritz crackers
I Surrender All	Carrots / baby carrots
I Want to be Mistaken for Jesus	Tomatoes / cherry tomatoes

Stripes

My family moved to northern Michigan when I was in tenth grade. We visited Calvary Bible Church and quickly decided that it would be our home church. Also attending were two elderly sisters, Lucille and Eileen All. They never married and they devoted their lives to God and to the church. Lucille taught a children's Sunday school class and Eileen was the Sunday School Secretary. I remember watching them receive awards every year for perfect attendance. Eileen received an award for 20 years of perfect attendance!

One Sunday morning Lucille led my sister Robin in prayer to accept Jesus as her personal Savior. I wonder how many other children did the same thing while in her class. I do know that these two women touched many lives. Every baby born to a family in church received a pair of baby booties knitted by Lucille. Even when her eyesight was so poor that she was declared legally blind, she continued to knit, blessing others with the beautiful things she made. Lucille exemplified the woman in Proverbs:

> *She selects wool and flax and works with eager hands. (Proverbs 31:13)*

Whenever the opportunity arose to share a favorite verse, Lucille always quoted Isaiah 53:6. She said it was her favorite verse because it started and ended with her name!

> *All we like sheep have gone astray; we have turned every one to his own way; and the LORD hath laid on Him the iniquity of us all.*
> *(Isaiah 53:6 KJV)*

One Easter Sunday, our son Daniel awoke to find a string tied to his bed. He followed the string out the door, through the backyard and into the barn. There he found a small lamb. Cupcake was soft and adorable. She followed him everywhere he went. When he ran, she ran. When he stopped, she stopped. Months went by and she grew quite large. We learned that sheep are very needy animals. They are dirty and they smell. We also learned they are not very smart. When we tied her out to graze, if she turned away she would cry until we went out, lifted her up, and turned her around so she could see the house. It really is not a compliment when the Bible refers to us as sheep. So often, we turn away from God and go our own way…we wander into sin. Someone had to pay the penalty for our disobedience.

> *For the wages of sin is death. (Romans 6:23)*

While in elementary school, my dad punished me for something I did not do. Someone wrote "Ron loves Nancy" on a piece of furniture and no one would confess to being the guilty person. My dad took a piece of paper and made each of us write down a few words. He then compared our handwriting to that on the dresser and decided that I was guilty. I cried and tried to convince him of my innocence, but the case was closed. Consequently, I took someone else's punishment. It was much later that I learned about the punishment that Jesus took, not just for me, but also for the entire world.

> *He was despised and rejected by men, a man of sorrows, and familiar with suffering. Like one from whom men hide their faces He was despised, and we esteemed Him not. Surely he took up our infirmities and carried our sorrows, yet we considered him stricken by God, smitten by him, and afflicted. But he was pierced for our transgressions, He was crushed for our iniquities; the punishment that brought us peace was upon him, and by his wounds we are healed. (Isaiah 53:3-5)*

I was guilty and they punished Jesus. He willingly paid the penalty for my sin. Most of the people I know who watched <u>The Passion of the Christ</u> walked away with a deeper understanding of the pain Jesus endured through His arrest and crucifixion. He was beaten and tortured because He loved us. We are healed because of His stripes (wounds). With His death, He purchased our eternal life (Revelation 5:9).

> *He was oppressed and afflicted, yet he did not open his mouth; he was led like a lamb to the slaughter, and as a sheep before her shearers is silent, so he did not open his mouth. (Isaiah 53:7)*

He did not try to convince His accusers of His innocence or tell them they had the wrong man. He willingly took the punishment that belonged to us. The penalty for sin is eternal death. We cannot earn our way into heaven. Salvation is available to us only because Jesus died in our place. If we receive the gift of salvation, we no longer face an eternity in hell.

> *For it is by grace you have been saved, through faith--and this not from yourselves, it is the **gift** of God-- not by works, so that no one can boast. (Ephesians 2:8-9)*

> *...the **gift** of God is eternal life in Christ Jesus our Lord. (Romans 6:23)*

When we celebrate our birthdays, we usually receive presents. We neither pay for them nor work for them. They are gifts given to us by those who love us; we simply accept them. Salvation is a gift from God, given out of love. We cannot pay for it and we cannot work for it. We must simply accept it.

> *"For God so loved the world that he gave his one and only Son, that whoever believes in him shall not perish but have eternal life."*
> *(John 3:16)*

Study Questions

1. Like a sheep, how have you strayed from God?

2. What are the eternal consequences of your sin?

3. What can you do to pay for the penalty of your sin?

4. Who paid the penalty for your sin? How?

5. Think about the best gift you ever received. Is it difficult for you to receive gifts from others? Do you feel like you "owe" them something in return?

6. Are you still trying to earn or repay God for your salvation? If yes, how so?

Perhaps you have never accepted God's gift of salvation. Why wait any longer? It's as easy as A, B, C.

    a. Admit (Romans 3:10, 23)
    b. Be willing and Believe (Acts 16:31)
    c. Confess and Commit (Romans 10:9-10, I John 1:9)

7. We read many of these verses previously in the chapter called, "The Path." Write down a verse about salvation that you have memorized, or one that you commit to memorize this week.

Thought for the week:
He came to pay a debt He did not owe; because we owed a debt we could not pay.

Today we are using a rib stitch to represent "stripes." Row by row, you will see how the stripes draw closer to each other as the piece grows in length. It reminds us of our need to draw closer to God. If we spend time with Him, moment by moment, in conversation and study, we will grow closer to Him as our Savior, Father, and Friend. The pattern today stretches when pulled. It has no choice but to "go the distance."

Consider how far God went to demonstrate His love. He loved us enough to provide a perfect eternal life. Christ's sacrifice was the ultimate when he stretched His arms out and died for us. It could not have been more. He sacrificed His Son, yet we reap the benefits! Our selfish desires evaporate as we absorb the downpour of His love, mercy and grace. Are you willing to go the distance for Him, even if it means being stretched beyond your comfort zone?

Today's Pattern:

 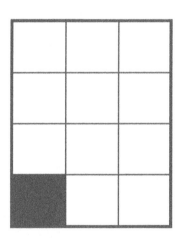

This is the "rib stitch." Gently pull the sides to expose the stripes and say, "By His stripes." Now let go and watch the ribs pull back together and say, "We are healed."

Directions:

Cast on 31

Knit 1 row

Increase row: Knit 1, (K1fb, Knit 1) repeat to the end. *(46 stitches)*

Row 1: Knit 2, (Purl 2, Knit 2) Repeat until 2 stitches remain and knit them.

Row 2: Knit 2, (Knit 2, Purl 2) Repeat until 2 stitches remain and knit them.

    Repeat Rows 1 and 2 until you near the desired length to form a square.

Decrease Row: (Knit 1, Knit 2 together) Repeat until 1 stitch remains and knit it. *(31 stitches)*

Knit 2 rows.

Bind off and weave in the loose ends. *(Optional: place safety pin)*

A new technique has been introduced today: Knitting into the front and back of a stitch (abbreviated "K1fb"). This is a way to increase the stitches without leaving an eyelet hole as we did in the previous chapter.

To K1fb, knit as usual into the stitch, but do not slip it off the needle: Instead, knit into the back of the same stitch. Once you have done this, slip the stitch completely off the needle, and you're done!

Troubleshooting Tips:

❖ Although the piece may appear large when you begin, it will pull together as you progress.

❖ How to tell when to knit and purl: the raised stitches are knit and the recessed stitches should be purled.

❖ After a few rows, you should be able to see the pattern form.

❖ I prefer to start the Decrease Row with the cast-on tail hanging on the right side, (along the same edge where you will begin knitting).

❖ Don't forget: the first and last two stitches of every row are knit to create the border.

Songs to knit by:	**Food for thought:**
Watch the Lamb	Keebler Striped cookies
He was Wounded for our	Candy Canes
Transgressions	Striped candy sticks
By His Wounds We Are Healed	Candy Corn

The Wordless Book

 I think I attended VBS just about every summer from the age of 6. I jumped at the opportunity whenever someone invited me along, and because many of our neighbors attended different churches, I was sometimes able to attend more than one session per summer. Then I entered Junior High School. As a seventh grader, I was too old to attend Vacation Bible School and my only consolation came when I was asked to be a teacher's helper. I eagerly rounded up all the little kids from the neighborhood and took them with me. I was no longer there just to have fun, but on a mission to see children saved. I paid close attention to the director as she talked about salvation, trying to remember every detail.

A few weeks later, the details I memorized came in handy. Our house had a partial basement and my parents wanted to expand it to the full size of our house. Along with my brother, they hired some neighborhood boys to dig out the rest of the basement. Now, because of my role as a teacher's helper, I was inspired to share the Gospel. I ventured down the basement steps to a captive audience (the only way out was to get past me and go up the stairs). I started by saying that I could show them how to go to heaven. They quit shoveling and listened. Then, I think I quoted John 3:16. I told them they needed to admit they were sinners and say the sinner's prayer, which I proceeded to quote. Everyone except my brother prayed with me. Feeling good about my little revival meeting, I headed back upstairs. That night at dinner, my brother informed my parents of the event. My mom told me I could not do that anymore because merely repeating a prayer did not save anyone. I was crushed. My days as a basement evangelist were over!

By the way, it is true that repeating a prayer does not save a person. There must also be a change of heart, a moment of surrendering your life to Christ. I guess the director of VBS failed to teach me that very important fact.

If you confess with your mouth, "Jesus is Lord," and believe in your heart that God raised him from the dead, you will be saved. For it is with your heart that you believe and are justified, and it is with your mouth that you confess and are saved. As the Scripture says, "Anyone who trusts in him will never be put to shame." For there is no difference between Jew and Gentile--the same Lord is Lord of all and richly blesses all who call on him, for, "Everyone who calls on the name of the Lord will be saved." (Romans 10:9-13)

Another lesson I learned at VBS was "The Wordless Book." This simple but ingenious idea uses colors to show God's plan of salvation. Let me share it with you.

It begins with a **BLACK** page. This page represents sin. According to Romans 3:23, everyone has sinned and fallen short of God's glory. We are in darkness, separated from God. There is nothing *we* can do to get out of the darkness or rid ourselves of sin.

> *...for all have sinned and fall short of the glory of God. (Romans 3:23)*

According to the Old Testament, a blood sacrifice was required for the atonement of sin. Jesus died in our place becoming the atonement for our sin, which is why the next color is **RED**; representing the blood of Jesus Christ (1 John 1:7).

> *He did not enter by means of the blood of goats and calves; but he entered the Most Holy Place once for all by his own blood, having obtained eternal redemption. (Hebrews 9:12)*

The **WHITE** page represents our sins washed white as snow! The moment we accept Christ as our Savior, the blood of Jesus cleanses us.

> *"Come now, let us reason together,"*
>   *says the LORD.*
> *"Though your sins are like scarlet,*
>   *they shall be as white as snow;*
> *though they are red as crimson,*
>   *they shall be like wool." (Isaiah 1:18)*

BLUE symbolizes the waters of baptism. Scripture tells us that baptism should happen after a person trusts in Christ, not before. Baptism symbolizes what happened inside the person. It is an act of obedience, an act of following Jesus' example.

> *But when they believed Philip as he preached the good news of the kingdom of God and the name of Jesus Christ, they were baptized, both men and women. (Acts 8:12)*

The **GREEN** page represents growth. Once we are saved, we need to grow in Christ. We do so by reading our Bibles, praying, going to church, and fellowshipping with other Christians.

> *But grow in the grace and knowledge of our Lord and Savior Jesus Christ. To him be glory both now and forever! (2 Peter 3:18)*

We end with **GOLD**, reminding us of the streets of gold in heaven. When we accept Christ as our Savior, we can rest assured we will spend eternity in heaven with Him. Can you imagine walking with Jesus down the streets of gold?

> *The great street of the city was of pure gold, like transparent glass. (Revelation 21:21)*

These six colors in book form have changed the lives of countless children and adults. It will continue to do so as long as we share it with others.

1. Is this the first time you've heard God's plan of salvation presented this way? If not, when did you first hear it?

2. How did you react?

3. Of the opportunities you had to share the Gospel, how many times were you obedient? Of the times you were disobedient, what kept you from sharing?

4. What will you do the next time you have an open door to share Christ? Begin praying about it now.

5. Consider using the Wordless Book. Its basic principles work with people of any age. Another way to lead people to Christ is the "Roman Road." All the verses come from the book of Romans. Let's walk down that road together by writing the following verses.

o   Romans 3:10

o   Romans 3:23

o   Romans 6:23a (first part of the verse)

o   Romans 6:23b (last part of the verse)

o   Romans 5:8

o   Romans 10:13

o   Romans 10:9-10

6. Reflect on the verses you have just written. Use this page to write down your thoughts.

Thought for the week:
"I asked Jesus how much he loved me. He stretched out his arms, said, '*This much*.' and then he died." Make a wordless book or use your finished square to share the story with a friend this week.

On the finished square, you will see a cross. Without Christ's love demonstrated upon the cross, we would be without hope because we cannot repay the debt of our sin. The bobbles placed on the cross remind us of our walk with Him: being rescued from our spiritual death and lifted to eternal life!

Today's Pattern:

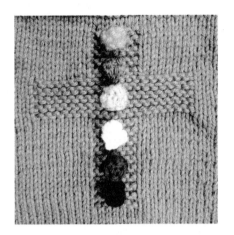
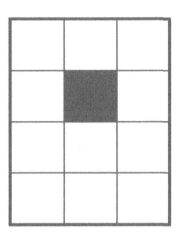

We were without hope because of our sin (black) and had no way of bridging the gap between God and us. Jesus Christ became our bridge. He came and paid our debt with His blood (red). His sacrifice made us pure (white) and blameless in God's eyes. We were given new life; we were born again. To show others of our commitment we are baptized (blue). Our walk with God is never-ending and He teaches us through the Bible and prayer to grow (green) in Him. When our journey on earth ends, we know that we will walk in His presence in Heaven (yellow).

Songs to knit by:
Old Rugged Cross
The Coloring Song: by Petra
Above All

Food for thought:
M&M's
Skittles
Jelly Beans

Directions:

Cast on 34

Knit 2 rows

Row 1: Knit

Row 2: Knit 2, Purl 30, Knit 2

Repeat Rows 1 and 2 one more time.

A: Knit across all stitches

B: Knit 2, Purl 12, Knit 6, Purl 12, Knit 2

Repeat A and B nine more times, (creating 10 ridges).

C: Knit across all stitches

D: Knit 2, Purl 5, Knit 20, Purl 5, Knit 2

Repeat Rows C and D four more times (this creates 5 ridges).

Now work rows A and B five times (this creates 5 ridges).

Work Rows 1 and 2 twice. (You can adjust the length by working these rows until the square is almost the desired length).

Knit 3 Rows

Bind off and weave in the loose ends. *(Optional: place safety pin)*

How to make the Bobbles:

You need 1 yard of yarn in: black, red, white, blue, green, and yellow.

Cast on 1 (being sure to leave a 6 inch tail).

K1fbf (You now have 3 stitches).

K1fb, Knit 1, K1fb (you now have 5 stitches).

Knit 2 rows

Knit 2 together, Knit 1, Knit 2 together (you now have 3 stitches).

Knit 3 together.

Use a tapestry needle to pull the yarn through the last loop remaining on the needle. Form the bobble into a ball shape and use the leftover yarn to sew it closed. Attach the bobble to the cross (as shown in the picture). Repeat the bobble pattern for each color of the wordless book.

Troubleshooting Tips:

❖ The cast on edge will try to roll upward.

❖ For "bobble" alternatives, please visit the members section of www.biblicalbits.com

❖ K1fb means Knit 1 into the front and back of the stitch. **K1fbf** means Knit 1 into the front, back and front of the stitch.

CAUTION:

Sew the bobbles on securely to prevent them from falling off during laundering. (This is especially important if you are making a baby blanket).

Hidden In My Heart

I have hidden your word in my heart that I might not sin against you. (Psalm 119:11)

Craig is my 42 year old brother-in-law. He is married to my sister Kathy and they have three children. A few years ago, Craig got involved with a Christian motorcycle group called H.I.M. (Hogs in Ministry) and has since worked his way up to "Road Captain." When I asked Craig how he received this honor, he told me about the requirements.

First, a prospective member must complete <u>The Change Workbook</u> which is based on Scripture and the changes Christ makes in your life. At the completion of this book, you may become a member of H.I.M. If you desire to advance into another part of the ministry, you have yet another workbook to complete. He said they encouraged him to memorize Scripture verses known as the Roman Road so that he could share Christ with others. Along with the title "Road Captain," he has the honor of leading the motorcycles when they go on ministry trips. By doing the workbooks, Craig is hiding God's Word in his heart.

But in your hearts set apart Christ as Lord. Always be prepared to give an answer to everyone who asks you to give the reason for the hope that you have. But do this with gentleness and respect. (1 Peter 3:15)

I often challenge women in our Bible study group to support what they are saying with Scripture. When they cannot, they flip open their Bibles and search for the answers. We are blessed to live in a country where we can own Bibles and openly worship God. I wonder, if we were suddenly without our Bibles, how much Scripture we would be able to pull from memory? Just how many Bible verses have we hidden in our heart? Jesus told us that the Holy Spirit would remind us of what He said.

*All this I have spoken while still with you. But the Counselor, the Holy Spirit, whom the Father will send in my name, will teach you all things and will **remind** you of everything I have said to you. (John 14:25-26)*

Notice the word "remind." We must first read the verses in order to be reminded of them. Too often people say that they cannot memorize Bible verses because their memory just isn't good enough. However, when asked what happened on their favorite television show, they give details of the current episode, as well as the previous week's episode. If they are capable of recalling television shows or singing along with the radio, they are capable of memorizing Scripture!

My husband gets frustrated because his memory is not as good as he would like it to be. Although he reads the Bible daily, he is concerned that he will not be able to remember a verse when he needs it. I believe that if he does his part by putting the verses into his heart, God will be faithful to remind him of them when necessary, just as He promised.

> *...the word is very near you; it is in your mouth and in your heart so you may obey it. (Deuteronomy 30:14)*

One morning while teaching a women's Sunday school class I felt a twinge in my leg. Sherri, who sat next to me, kicked me and it was not an accident. She deliberately kicked me! I glanced at her only to be given a funny look. I continued with the lesson, but when it was over, I asked her why she kicked me. Her reply, with a grin, was that she wished I had not taught how to keep our minds pure by being careful about the movies we watch and the books we read. As long as she remained ignorant about what God had to say about certain subjects, she thought she did not have to obey! Can you relate to Sherri? If you don't know the rules do you assume you don't have to follow them? Scripture is given to us so that we can obey God. Do you want to know how to be a good mother? Read the Bible. Do you want to know how to be a good wife? Do you want to know how to please God? Do you want to be a good businessperson? Read the Bible, hide His Word in your heart, obey Him, and watch God shower you with blessings as you trust Him to be faithful to His words in John 14:25-26.

1. Write any verses that you have memorized.

2. Who reminds us of the Scripture we read?

3. Have you had an experience when the correct Scripture came to mind just when you needed it?

4. Has someone given you a passage of Scripture when you needed to hear it? Explain.

5. Why is it important to memorize Scripture?

6. Do we continue to sin because we have failed to hide God's Word in our heart?

7. Are you accountable to God if you don't know all the rules? Why? (Deut. 12:32)

Here are some ways to begin hiding God's Word in your heart.

- Keep your Bible near you and meditate on the Word throughout the day.
- Heed this advice from Psalms 46:10 *"Be still, and know that I am God..."*
- Try to settle down and clear your mind before you start.
- Begin by praying, asking God to teach you what He wants you to learn.
- Listen to what God is saying.
- Write the verse you wish to memorize on an index card. Carry it with you, looking at it often during the day.
- Start and end your day by reading the verse and then trying to recite it.
- If you have children or grandchildren, encourage them to memorize verses with you. They too will hear the God's Word and you will appreciate the competition!

8. Which verse will you commit to memorizing this week? Begin by writing it.

Thought for the week:
Whether through a Church program, a neighborhood Bible study, or working on your own, start memorizing Scripture. The rewards are out of this world!

We cannot expect to keep Scripture hidden within if we do not expose ourselves to it daily. The Bible is the most valuable book we possess.

> *All Scripture is God-breathed and is useful for teaching, rebuking, correcting and training in righteousness. (2 Timothy 3:16)*

Today we are using a needle and yarn to attach two knitted pieces together. Together they form a pocket in which to hold God's Word. Using a small Bible, bookmark a verse that you need to memorize, or highlight the "Romans Road" you learned in last week's lesson. (Romans 3:10, 3:23, 6:23, 5:8, 10:13, 10:9-10).

Today's Pattern:

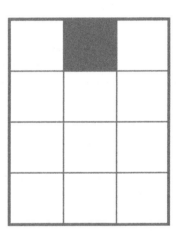

Hold a small Bible (or New Testament) and as you place it in the pocket, say, "*I have hidden Your Word in my heart*" (Look at the heart and remember why we keep Scripture stored there), "*that I might not sin against You.*" (Psalm 119:11)

Directions:

To Make the Background:
Knit a square in Garter Stitch (see Pattern 1 on page 18) or Stockinette Stitch (Pattern 2 on page 24) and set it aside.

To Make the Pocket:
Cast on 22 then work the Seed Stitch Border as follows:
(Knit 1, Purl 1) repeat to the end.
(Purl 1, Knit 1) repeat to the end.
Repeat these 2 rows again.

Row 1: Knit 1, Purl 1, Knit 19, Purl 1
Row 2: Purl 1, Knit 1, Purl 19, Knit 1
Repeat Rows 1 and 2 one more time.
Row 3: Knit 1, Purl 1, Knit 8, Purl 2, Knit 9, Knit 1
Row 4 AND ALL EVEN NUMBERED ROWS *through Row 22*: **Purl 1, Knit 1, Purl 19, Knit 1.**
Row 5: Knit 1, Purl 1, Knit 7, Purl 4, Knit 8, Purl 1
Row 7: Knit 1, Purl 1, Knit 6, Purl 6, Knit 7, Purl 1
Row 9: Knit 1, Purl 1, Knit 5, Purl 8, Knit 6, Purl 1,
Row 11: Knit 1, Purl 1, Knit 4, Purl 10, Knit 5, Purl 1
Row 13: Knit 1, Purl 1, Knit 3, Purl 12, Knit 4, Purl 1
Row 15: Knit 1, Purl 1, Knit 2, Purl 14, Knit 3, Purl 1
Row 17: Repeat Row 15 two more times.
Row 19: Knit 1, Purl 1, Knit 3, Purl 5, Knit 2, Purl 5, Knit 4, Purl 1
Row 21: Knit 1, Purl 1, Knit 4, Purl 3, Knit 4, Purl 3, Knit 5, Purl 1
Row 23-26: Work Rows 1 and 2 twice.
Rows 27-29: Work in the Rib Stitch: (Knit 1, Purl 1) across all stitches.
Bind off and weave in the loose ends. *(Optional: place safety pin)*

Sew the pocket to the center of the square using a yarn needle and matching yarn. You can outline the heart in the contrasting color. (Visit our website for information on the duplicate stitch and other techniques).

Troubleshooting Tips:
❖ Use a row counter to keep track or your place in the pattern.

❖ Pay close attention to the directions of Row 4 as you knit.

<u>Songs to knit by:</u>	<u>Food for thought:</u>
Remember Me: sung by Mark Schultz	Testamints
Thy Word	Heart shaped cookies
The B-I-B-L-E	Conversation hearts

Trinity

Several years ago, my husband and I were discussing the toys we had as children. He told me he got a Johnny Seven Gun for Christmas when he was ten years old and it was the best gift he ever received. I tried to imagine what this seven-in-one gun looked like. The Johnny Seven could fire four different types of bullets and rockets and came complete with a grenade, launcher, and tripod. With the push of a button, a pistol slid out of the bottom and fired caps. His face lit up as he remembered all the fun times he had playing Army with his brothers.

Two years ago while searching for an out-of-print book I decided to check eBay. One thing led to another and before I knew it, I started looking for that gun. Lo and behold, I found a Johnny Seven Gun! Once I saw what it looked like, I realized why he described it as seven guns in one. I clicked the listing and to my amazement the bid was up to $350.00. As much as I wanted to buy it, I knew it was out of my price range so my search continued. I found several auctions that offered parts of the gun. Over the next three months, I purchased enough broken guns to piece together a complete one. I guess you really can say it is seven (or eight) guns in one! On my husband's 48th birthday the gift overwhelmed him. We laughed as he launched rockets and reminisced of days gone by.

I had a hard time trying to understand a seven-in-one gun. Imagine my difficultly in trying to understand the Trinity! Although I heard several knowledgeable people describe the trinity, I still found it a concept difficult to grasp. Let's look at Scripture and see what the Bible has to say.

- There is one and only one eternal God. The Trinity does not mean that there are three gods.

  Hear, O Israel: The LORD our God, **the LORD is one.**
  (Deuteronomy 6:4)

- There are three eternal Persons: the Father, the Son, and the Holy Spirit.

  Therefore go and make disciples of all nations, baptizing them in the name of the **Father** *and of the* **Son** *and of the* **Holy Spirit.**
  (Matthew 28:19)

*For through **him** (Jesus) we both have access to the **Father** by one **Spirit**. (Ephesians 2:18)*

- The Bible identifies the Father, the Son, and the Holy Spirit as being God.

  *Grace, mercy and peace from **God the Father**. (2 John 1:3)*

  *In the beginning was the Word, and the Word was with God, and **the Word was God.** He was with God in the beginning...**The Word became flesh** (Jesus) and made his dwelling among us. We have seen his glory, the glory of the One and Only, who came from the Father, full of grace and truth. (John 1:1-2, 14)*

  *"...while we wait for the blessed hope-the glorious appearing of our great **God and Savior, Jesus Christ**... (Titus 2:13)*

  In Acts 5:3-4 Peter confronts Ananias about lying to the **Holy Spirit** and finishes by telling Ananias that he has lied to **God**.

- God does not change, He has always existed as He does today; One God- 3 persons.

  Jesus Christ is the same yesterday and today and forever. (Hebrews 13:8)

  Every good and perfect gift is from above, coming down from the Father of the heavenly lights, who does not change like shifting shadows. (James 1:7)

Although the word "Trinity" does not appear in the Bible, we do see it in verses such as:

  *Then **God** said, "Let us make man in **our** image, in **our** likeness..." (Genesis 1:26)*

  *Therefore go and make disciples of all nations, baptizing them in the name of the **Father** and of the **Son** and of the **Holy Spirit**. (Matthew 28:19)*

  ***He** saved us, not because of righteous things we had done, but because of his mercy. He saved us through the washing of rebirth and renewal by the **Holy Spirit**, whom he poured out on us generously through **Jesus Christ** our Savior. (Titus 3:5-6)*

*As soon as Jesus was baptized, he went up out of the water. At that moment heaven was opened, and he saw the **Spirit of God** descending like a dove and lighting on him. And a **voice from heaven** said, "This is my **Son**, whom I love; with him I am well pleased." (Matthew 3:16-17)*

Christians take comfort in the Trinity, realizing that God never changes. The Father loves us, the Son died for us, and the Holy Spirit lives within us. We serve a God who loved us so much that He came to dwell among us, He came to dwell within us, and when our work on earth is finished, we will dwell within His presence.

Study Questions

1. What is the definition of 'Trinity"?

2. How many times does the word "Trinity" appear in the Bible?

3. Who are the three Persons that make up the Trinity?

4. What does the word eternal mean?

5. Which person of the Trinity became flesh?

6. How is Jesus described in John 1:1?

7. When did the Holy Spirit come into existence?

To answer this question, please review the following:

    a. Is the Holy Spirit God?

    b. Does God ever change?

    c. When did God come into existence?

8. Based on Psalm 90: 2, how would you answer question 7?

9. Write a list of questions that you have about the Trinity:

10. Compile a list of sources (books, websites, and people) that you will use to find the answers to your questions above.

Thought for the week:
When he went to Ireland to tell the people about God, St. Patrick used a shamrock to illustrate the trinity. The three petals represented the Father, Son, and Holy Spirit: three Persons — one God.

Pattern 11: Trinity Stitch

The Trinity stitch brings three stitches together as one. While you work on this project, let each "Knit, Purl, Knit into 1 stitch" remind you of the Father, Son, and Holy Spirit as one God. Your mind might run in circles at the thought of the Trinity, because it is unique, complex, and unseen.

You may find the same thoughts entering your mind as you attempt today's pattern. It challenges the knitter with steps like "purl 3 stitches together." Think of it as a new dance step for your fingers. With a little practice, you will waltz your way through it. If you have "two left hands" and find this dance too difficult, please visit our website for assistance.

Today's Pattern:

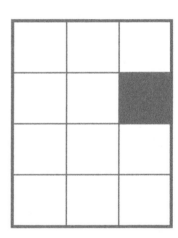

Each bobble was formed with three stitches joined together as one; a reminder of the Trinity: Father, Son, and Holy Spirit- three persons, but one God.

Directions:

Cast on 34

Knit 1 Row

Increase Row: Knit 2, (K1fb, Knit 4) Repeat until 2 stitches remain and Knit them. (*There should be 40 stitches on your needle*)

Knit 1 row

Row 1: Knit 2, *(Knit, Purl, Knit into one stitch), Purl 3 together. Repeat from the * until 2 stitches remain and knit them.

Row 2: Knit 2, Purl 36, Knit 2

Row 3: Knit 2, *Purl 3 together, (Knit, Purl, and Knit into one stitch). Repeat from the * until 2 stitches remain and knit them.

Row 4: Knit 2, Purl 36, Knit 2

Repeat Rows 1-4 nine times or until you have almost reached the desired length to form a square.

Decrease Row: When you get to Row 4, replace it with: (Knit 4, Knit 2 together) Repeat what is in the parentheses until 4 stitches remain and knit them. (*34 stitches*)

Knit 2 rows.

Bind off and weave in the loose ends. (*Optional: place safety pin*)

Troubleshooting Tips:

❖ K1fb means Knit 1 into the front AND back of the stitch.

❖ The "repeat" on Rows 1 and 3 is a bit different than what you may be used to because you will repeat more than just what is in the parentheses.

❖ To Purl 3 stitches together, position the tip of your "working" knitting needle towards the ceiling as you pull the yarn through all three stitches.

❖ If you tried and tried but can't get a certain row to turn out correctly, you have probably made an error in the previous row(s).

❖ Remember to visit our website for additional help and pattern updates.

Songs to knit by:	Food for thought:
He is the Alpha and Omega	Cloverleaf rolls
The Doxology	Shamrock cookies
I Am (by Mark Schultz)	Three Musketeers
Holy, Holy, Holy	

Honeycomb

Around the time, our son, Daniel, graduated from high school, my husband decided to plant a few apple trees. Summer graduated the following year and he planted more apple trees along with a few cherry trees. Two years later our youngest child, Sarah, graduated and low and behold, the size of our orchard increased. Now, ten years later our little orchard is home to approximately seventy-five fruit trees. Last year he informed me that we needed a beehive. "Bees," he said, "are necessary to pollinate the blossoms. The more blossoms pollinated, the larger the harvest of fruit." I don't know very much about bees, but I do know that they sting! Trying to convince me of its necessity, he enticed me with the thought of having our own supply of honey. That caused me to think of him in a beekeeper's suit, which made me chuckle. He convinced me. The new addition to the orchard this year will be a beehive.

While driving to our house, Summer and Ken stopped at a farmer's roadside stand where they purchased one pint of golden honey. Much to their dismay, when they opened it, the smell was so bad that they could not eat it. The smell and flavor of honey depends on where the bees collect the pollen. If you want good, sweet honey, it must come from good, sweet pollen.

Samson found honey inside the carcass of a lion. I can only imagine how it smelled and I do not even want to imagine how it tasted. What I would like to know is why in the world Samson approached a dead lion! As a Nazirite, he took special vows before the Lord. One such vow prohibited him from being in the presence of dead things. Samson looked for something good and sweet inside something dead.

> *He turned aside to look at the lion's carcass. In it was a swarm of bees and some honey, which he scooped out with his hands and ate as he went along. When he rejoined his parents, he gave them some, and they too ate it. But he did not tell them that he had taken the honey from the lion's carcass. (Judges 14:8-9)*

So often, we, like Samson, look for sweet things in places we do not belong. We try and convince ourselves that in certain circumstances, the good outweighs the bad. Take, for instance, movies. Despite the rating it received because of nudity and language, we feel that the story itself is good, and the nudity and language will not really affect us. Kids use the same logic with music. They tell us that they don't really listen to the words; they just like the beat. Christians do it when they date unsaved people. They convince themselves that by dating him/her they will be a good influence and draw them to the Lord. We are to be kind and witness to unsaved people, but God tells us we are to be **in** the world, but not **of** the world (John 14:14-18). The list could go on and on but let's face it, we are no better than Samson, thinking we can get something good out of something dead. We think that we can get close to dead or unclean things and come out unscathed. Whom are we kidding? Certainly not God! Do you ever wonder why you feel uneasy when you do these things? Listen to what the Bible says about peace.

Finally, brothers, whatever is true, whatever is noble, whatever is right, whatever is pure, whatever is lovely, whatever is admirable--if anything is excellent or praiseworthy--think about such things. Whatever you have learned or received or heard from me, or seen in me--put it into practice. And the God of peace will be with you. (Philippians 4:8-9)

When harvesting honey, the beekeeper must wear the proper attire to avoid painful stings. The bees put a lot of hard work into producing the honey and they are not thrilled with the idea of someone invading their territory to take the fruits of their labor. Once he reaches the hive, the beekeeper must remove the racks containing the honeycomb. He then warms the honeycomb and extracts the honey. Most of us know that honey is very sweet. It only takes a small amount to sweeten a cup of tea. To me, that little bit of sweetness makes a big difference in the taste. According to Scripture, God's Word is even sweeter than honey.

How sweet are your words to my taste, sweeter than honey to my mouth!
(Psalm 119:103)

The fear of the LORD is pure, enduring forever.
The ordinances of the LORD are sure and altogether righteous.
They are more precious than gold, than much pure gold;
They are sweeter than honey, than honey from the comb.
(Psalm 19:9-10)

When we read the Bible, it should taste good and bring nourishment to our soul. I am so glad that we do not have to dress in special clothes, risk painful injury, or wait for someone else to extract it, in order to enjoy the sweetness of the Word of God. Sometimes though, we act as if it is work.

We give all kinds of excuses why we cannot read the Bible. Perhaps we fear that the Bible is beyond our understanding, so we should not we even attempt to read it. Often we fail to see the value of Scripture. Reading and meditating on God's Word helps us to make wise choices.

Dead or unclean things are not quite as appealing after you have spent time with the Lord. Set aside whatever excuses you have for not reading the Bible and begin the wonderful journey of getting to know our Lord and Savior. He desires to spend time with you. He never changes and His promises never fail, so take comfort in His Word.

> *The LORD himself goes before you and will be with you; he will never leave you nor forsake you. Do not be afraid; do not be discouraged. (Deuteronomy 3:18)*
>
> *I have loved you with an everlasting love;*
> *I have drawn you with loving-kindness. (Jeremiah 31:3)*

1. Samson looked for something sweet inside something dead. In what areas of life do you face the same struggle?

Put on the full armor of God so that you can take your stand against the devil's schemes. For our struggle is not against flesh and blood, but against the rulers, against the authorities, against the powers of this dark world and against the spiritual forces of evil in the heavenly realms. Therefore put on the full armor of God, so that when the day of evil comes, you may be able to stand your ground, and after you have done everything, to stand. Stand firm then, with the belt of truth buckled around your waist, with the breastplate of righteousness in place, and with your feet fitted with the readiness that comes from the gospel of peace. In addition to all this, take up the shield of faith, with which you can extinguish all the flaming arrows of the evil one. Take the helmet of salvation and the sword of the Spirit, which is the word of God. And pray in the Spirit on all occasions with all kinds of prayers and requests. With this in mind, be alert and always keep on praying for all the saints. (Ephesians 6:11-18)

2. Why should we put on the full armor of God?

3. What does the belt represent?

4. What does the breastplate represent?

5. With what are our feet to be fitted?

6. Why do we need the shield of faith?

7. What is the helmet?

8. What is the sword of the Spirit?

9. What should we do after we put on the armor (verse 18)?

10. Are you making wise choices? How do you know? Write Philippians 4:8 on an index card and place it above your television, radio, or phone.

11. God's Word is sweet. Are you taking time to read it as discussed in the "Hidden in my Heart "section? What steps have you taken to read God's Word more regularly? Won't you make it a priority in your life?

Your word is a lamp to my feet and a light for my path. I have taken an oath and confirmed it, that I will follow your righteous laws.
(Psalm 119:105-106)

Thought for the week:
Grab a cup of tea, sweetened with honey. Snuggle up with your new Story Blanket and your Bible. Open to the book of Psalms and heed the words in chapter 34: ***"Taste and see that the LORD is good."***

Pattern 12: Honeycomb Stitch

Sometimes we find ourselves in places we don't belong, both physically and mentally. Today's square, The Honeycomb, reminds us to stay away from "sticky" situations. The pattern requires focus, just as God's commands us to be focused on Him. You will also be using an extra needle called a "cabling needle." The pattern is difficult without it. This reminds us of how we too can benefit from something extra: other Christians. Their involvement in our lives can offer godly council and accountability.

Today's Pattern:

 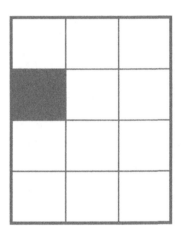

When the pattern is finished, you will see the honeycomb. It is a reminder to avoid sticky situations. Do you see the holes within the finished square? They remind us of the holes we dig by getting involved where we do not belong; we will stumble and fall into them. Only God can pull us out, forgive us, and place us where we need to be. He is something sweeter that we should seek (Psalm 19:7-11).

Directions:

Cast on 34

Knit 1 row

Increase row: Knit 3, (Knit 1, K1fb) repeat what is in the parentheses until 3 stitches remain and knit them. *(48 stitches)*

Row 1: Knit

Row 2: Knit 2, Purl 44, Knit 2

Row 3: Knit 2, (Slip the first 2 stitches onto the extra needle and let it lay on the **back** of your piece. Knit 2 stitches off the left needle. Now, knit the stitches off the extra needle. Slip the next 2 stitches onto the extra needle and let it lay in **front** of your piece. Knit 2 stitches off the left needle. Now, knit the stitches off the extra needle). Repeat what is in the parentheses until 2 stitches remain and knit them.

Row 4: Knit 2, Purl 44, Knit 2

Row 5: Knit

Row 6: Knit 2, Purl 44, Knit 2

Row 7: Knit 2, (Slip 2 stitches onto the extra needle and lay it in **front** of your work. Knit 2 stitches off the left needle. Knit the stitches on the extra needle. Slip the next 2 stitches onto the extra needle and let it lay on the **back** of your piece. Knit 2 stitches off the left needle. Now knit the stitches off the extra needle). Repeat what is in the parentheses until 2 stitches remain and knit them.

Row 8: Knit 2, Purl 44, Knit 2

Repeat Rows 1-8 until the desired length is almost reached.

Decrease Row: On Row 1 or Row 5, with the right side facing you, Knit 2, (Knit 1, Knit 2 together) repeat what is in the parentheses until 4 stitches remain and knit them. *(You should have 34 stitches on your needle now).*

Knit 2 rows

Bind off and weave in the loose ends. *(Optional: place safety pin)*

Troubleshooting Tips:

❖ If you do not have a cabling needle, find something else to use or visit our website to see how to cable without a needle. The cabling needle simply holds the stitches until you need them again.

❖ I begin and end the bind off row by knitting 2 together. This helps the top edge to stay in proportion to the rest of the square. You may not need to do this, especially if you are a tight knitter.

Songs to knit by:	Food for thought:
Oh Taste and See	Honeycomb cereal
'Tis so Sweet to Trust in Jesus	Honey-butter and biscuits
The law of the Lord is perfect	Bit o' Honey candy

Finishing Technique

Right now you have 12 squares in front of you and perhaps you're feeling a bit overwhelmed, asking yourself, "Now what?" I've been there too! Finishing techniques and knitting share similar qualities: they must be learned and perfected. However, let me pass along a few tips I've learned throughout my challenges, so as to make your experience a bit easier.

First, "block" your squares. Blocking isn't necessary, but helpful. I prefer to pin the squares that need re-shaping to the ironing board and spritz them with water or steam. This is a great way to tame those stubborn stockinette squares! The squares dry in the shape you have pinned them. Once dry, remove the pieces from the ironing board.

Seed	Hidden in My Heart	Increase/ Decrease
Honeycomb	The Cross	Trinity
Stockinette	The Path	Garter
Stripes	Square	Basketweave

Lay out your 12 squares as diagramed on page 10. Check to ensure the "right side" (pretty, patterned side) of each is facing you. Tip: Arrange them so that the cast on "tail" (or safety pin as advised in Pattern 1) lies at the bottom right corner of each square.

You are now ready to piece your blanket together by sewing one section at a time. I prefer to start by joining the left column to the middle column, working from the bottom to the top, creating one vertical seam.

To do this, cut a length of yarn 3 x the length of the blanket. Thread your yarn needle with coordinating yarn and stitch through the corner of the left side square (the "Stripes" pattern) and then through closest corner of the right side square (the "Square Stitch" pattern).

Continue seaming the pieces together, stitching from the garter stitch border of the left, to the garter stitch border on the right, keeping your tension consistent as you go. Because your squares may not be the exact same length, you may need to skip a row of stitches on one side to keep the squares even in length as you progress towards the top.

When you finish seaming the first two squares, continue by adding the next two, until you arrive at the top of the blanket. I use safety pins to hold the squares together at the points where four squares meet. This puts less strain on the yarn as you progress towards the top of the blanket. Weave in the tail and trim off the excess.

Now connect the middle section to the right column in the same manner as before (this time attaching the "Square Stitch," to the "Basketweave" square). Continue to the top of the blanket, remembering to weave in and trim the excess yarn when you are finished.

Using the same technique, sew the remaining open seams. Start at the bottom left side and connect the top of the "Stripes" square to the bottom of the "Stockinette" square. Sew across the row and finish by weaving in the loose ends and trimming off the excess yarn. Repeat the process with the middle and top row.

The Border

The border isn't difficult, but it is time consuming because it must be sewn to the blanket upon completion. Many people choose to crochet a border, but for those of you who would rather knit, this pattern is for you. (As a bonus- there is no purling!)

Cast on 9 using whichever color yarn you prefer for the border.

Row 1: Knit 3, (yarn over, Knit 2 together) Repeat twice, Knit 2.
Row 2: Knit 4, (yarn over, Knit 2 together) Repeat twice, Knit 1.
Row 3: Knit 3, (yarn over, Knit 2 together) Repeat twice, Knit 1, K1fb.
Row 4: Knit 5, (yarn over, Knit 2 together) Repeat twice, Knit 1.
Row 5: Knit 3, (yarn over, Knit 2 together) Repeat twice, Knit 2, K1fb.
Row 6: Knit 6, (yarn over, Knit 2 together) Repeat twice, Knit 1.
Row 7: Knit 3, (yarn over, Knit 2 together) Repeat twice, Knit 3, **K1fbf**.
Row 8: Knit 3 together, Knit 5, (yarn over, Knit 2 together) Repeat twice, Knit 1.
Row 9: Knit 3, (yarn over, Knit 2 together) Repeat twice, Knit 2, Knit 2 together.
Row 10: Knit 5, (yarn over, Knit 2together) Repeat twice, Knit 1.
Row 11: Knit 3, (yarn over, Knit 2 together) Repeat twice, Knit 1, Knit 2 together.
Row 12: Knit 4, (yarn over, Knit 2 together) Repeat twice, Knit 1.

Repeat Rows 1-12 until the border is long enough to be attached to the perimeter of the blanket and bind off.

Hints: The first time you knit the "funny stitch" (the yarn over from the previous row), it's a cue to "yarn over, Knit 2 together."

Using a yarn needle, sew the flat edge of the border to the edge of the blanket. Finish by sewing the bind off edge to the cast on edge and weave in the loose ends.

You can knit a portion of the border and attach it, continuing to knit and sew as you go.

Abbreviations:
K1fb: Knit into the front and back of the stitch (Makes 2 stitches).
K1fbf: Knit into the front, back, and front again of the stitch (Makes 3 stitches).

Conclusion

Harold was my friend. I met him because of a Children's Literature class I took at the local community college. My children were away at college and I thought I would enjoy taking a couple of classes too. The professor told the class that we had to put in several hours at an elementary school reading to the children. Having taught kindergarten at a Christian school, I had plenty of experience reading to children so I asked if I could read to nursing home residents instead.

The recreational director at the nursing home arranged for me to read to the residents who did not receive many visitors. Since there were no special requirements regarding which books I could read, I always included the Bible. I was amazed at how hearing the Word of God touched the residents; the book of Psalms was always a favorite, usually moving the residents to tears. They took such comfort in hearing of God's unfailing love. As I sat in the community room reading to them, I often saw an elderly man named Harold sitting in the corner with his head down. Apparently, when asked if he would like me to read to him, he declined.

One afternoon I walked over and asked him if he ever went hunting. He nodded his head, indicating that he had. I told him about the seven-point buck I took the previous day. He lifted his head and for the first time, looked at me. After I gave him the details of my bow-hunting experience, I asked him if he would like to see a picture. He nodded his head yes. I said that I would bring one the next time I came in; I added that I would be happy to bring a book with fishing stories if he was interested. Once again, he nodded his head.

On my next visit, Harold held the picture and did not want to give it back.
"Would you like to keep it for a while?" I asked him.
"Yes." He replied. His voice was barely audible.
I left the picture in his hands and I began to read to him.

Harold and I visited every Tuesday and Thursday. He listened as I read stories about fishing and hunting and more importantly, he listened as I read the Bible. Tears flowed from his eyes when I read passages of God's love for him.

One Tuesday, Harold was not in the community room. The director told me that he was sick but I could go to his room and see him. I had never been in Harold's room. I walked in to find him in bed, covered with an oxygen tent. As I stood next to him and looked around, the only picture on his bulletin board was the picture of me with the deer. The only book he had was the fishing book I gave him.

Harold opened his eyes and looked at me. This time there were no hunting and fishing stories. I picked up my Bible and read from the book of Psalms and when I finished I asked Harold if I could pray with him. He nodded his head. I lifted the oxygen tent enough so that I could hold his hand; I prayed that God would heal him and make him strong. As I released his hand, I told Harold I would see him Thursday.

When I arrived at the nursing home on Thursday the director asked me to come in her office. She told me that Harold had passed away. She handed me my picture and my book. I took them and went home.

Months later, I met someone who had known Harold. I made the comment that I really did not know anything about him. She told me that Harold was a drunk and was very abusive to his wife and family; no one loved him, and no one wanted to be around him.

I am so glad that I did not know about Harold's past when he was alive. I can be very judgmental and if I knew about the things he did, I may have shunned him like everyone else and I would have missed the blessing of his friendship. My hope is that Harold accepted Christ's forgiveness and is in heaven with God.

There are people like Harold in every community. No one wants to visit them, no one cares about them, and no one loves them. No one, that is, except God. Remember, Jesus died for them too. They need to hear about God's love and forgiveness and you have the tools to give them the good news of Jesus Christ. Take your Story Blanket and your Bible and find someone like Harold in your neighborhood. Sit with them, read to them, talk with them and tell them the story behind the squares in your Story Blanket, but beware! You may find yourself developing friendships you never thought possible!

We pray that you will continue to study God's Word and share what you learn with others. Please let us know how God is working in your life.

~ Vicki Bedford

Congratulations Knit-Wits! I hope you enjoyed your knitting journey, but I pray that it does not end here. You are holding a tool of ministry, your Story Blanket. Each piece reminds us of what our Savior did for us, and what we can do to grow in Him. Pray and ask God how He can use you to continue His work in sharing Jesus with others.

Consider ministering to the blind. Each of the squares has a distinct feel. Let their hands follow the "pages" of the Story Blanket as you describe each one. Spend time getting to know the person/people. Take along your Biblical Bits for Knit-Wits book and ask if you can share it with them.

Perhaps you are giving your Story Blanket as a gift. Place a small Bible in the pocket and highlight verses that have encouraged or challenged you. Maybe these are verses about His love, peace during the storm, salvation, or forgiveness. Perhaps you'll highlight the verses of the "Romans Road." Be sure to bookmark Psalm 139:13-14 as a reminder that we were created with a purpose and plan.

Seek out someone who needs to know that God and you care for them. Knit a Story Blanket for that person and share the story behind it. Attach a card to the finished product that says:

> *"Wrapped in love, covered in prayer;*
> *Wherever you are, God is there."*
>
> *Wrap this around your shoulders and know that it*
> *is a hug from me whenever you need it.*

Consider knitting a few Story Blankets and donating them to your local Crisis Pregnancy Center. How wonderful to gift your blanket to a mother who may not know that God lovingly knit her child together. The blanket that holds her child securely also tells of the security offered in Christ.

If you choose to keep your Story Blanket, display it where it will be seen and used. Explain the meaning of each square with neighbors, friends, visitors, and family. Younger children love hearing stories repeated time and time again. Ask them to point out their favorite square and tell you what it represents. This is an effective way to teach them Scripture that they can hide in their heart! I look forward to hearing how God uses you and your story Blanket for His glory. May God bless you and your ministry.

~ Summer Mungle

Steps to Peace with God

By Billy Graham

Step 1: GOD'S PURPOSE: PEACE AND LIFE

God loves you and wants you to experience peace and life—abundant and eternal. The Bible says ...

"We have peace with God through our Lord Jesus Christ." — *Romans 5:1 (NIV)*

"For God so loved the world that He gave His only begotten Son, that whoever believes in Him should not perish but have everlasting life." — *John 3:16 (NIV)*

"I have come that they may have life, and that they may have it more abundantly." — *John 10:10 (NIV)*

Step 2: THE PROBLEM: OUR SEPARATION

God created us in His own image to have an abundant life. He did not make us as robots to automatically love and obey Him. God gave us a will and a freedom of choice.
We chose to disobey God and go our own willful way. We still make this choice today. This results in separation from God. The Bible says ...

"For all have sinned and fall short of the glory of God." — *Romans 3:23 (NIV)*

"For the wages of sin is death, but the gift of God is eternal life in Christ Jesus our Lord." — *Romans 6:23 (NIV)*

Our Attempts to Reach God
People have tried in many ways to bridge this gap between themselves and God. The Bible says ...

"There is a way that seems right to a man, but in the end it leads to death." — *Proverbs 14:12 (NIV)*

"But your iniquities have separated you from your God; your sins have hidden his face from you, so that he will not hear." — *Isaiah 59:2 (NIV)*

No bridge reaches God ... except one.

Step 3: GOD'S BRIDGE: THE CROSS

Jesus Christ died on the Cross and rose from the grave. He paid the penalty for our sin and bridged the gap between God and people. The Bible says ...

"For there is one God and one mediator between God and men, the man Jesus Christ."
— 1 Timothy 2:5 (NIV)

"For Christ died for sins once for all, the righteous for the unrighteous, to bring you to God."
— 1 Peter 3:18 (NIV)

"But God demonstrates his own love for us in this: While we were still sinners, Christ died for us."
— Romans 5:8 (NIV)

God has provided the only way. Each person must make a choice.

Step 4: OUR RESPONSE: RECEIVE CHRIST

We must trust Jesus Christ as Lord and Savior and receive Him by personal invitation. The Bible says ...

"Here I am! I stand at the door and knock. If anyone hears my voice and opens the door, I will come in and eat with him, and he with me." Revelation 3:20 (NIV)

"Yet to all who received him, to those who believed in his name, he gave the right to become children of God." John 1:12 (NIV)

"That if you confess with your mouth, 'Jesus is Lord,' and believe in your heart that God raised Him from the dead, you will be saved." Romans 10:9 (NIV)

Where are you?
Will you receive Jesus Christ right now?

Here is how you can receive Christ:
1. Admit your need (I am a sinner).
2. Be willing to turn from your sins (repent).
3. Believe that Jesus Christ died for you on the Cross and rose from the grave.
4. Through prayer, invite Jesus Christ to come in and control your life through the Holy Spirit.
(Receive Him as Lord and Savior.)

How to Pray:

Dear Lord Jesus, I know that I am a sinner and need Your forgiveness. I believe that You died for my sins. I want to turn from my sins. I now invite You to come into my heart and life. I want to trust and follow You as Lord and Savior. In Jesus' name. Amen.

God's Assurance: His Word

If you prayed this prayer, The Bible says ...

"Everyone who calls on the name of the Lord will be saved." Romans 10:13 (NIV)

Did you sincerely ask Jesus Christ to come into your life? Where is He right now? What has He given you?

"For it is by grace you have been saved, through faith — and this not from yourselves, it is the gift of God — not by works, so that no one can boast." Ephesians 2:8-9 (NIV)

Receiving Christ, we are born into God's family through the supernatural work of the Holy Spirit who indwells every believer. This is called regeneration, or the "new birth."

This is just the beginning of a wonderful new life in Christ. To deepen this relationship you should:

1. Read your Bible everyday to know Christ better.
2. Talk to God in prayer every day.
3. Tell others about Christ.
4. Worship, fellowship, and serve with other Christians in a church where Christ is preached.
5. As Christ's representative in a needy world, demonstrate your new life by your love and concern for others.

Made in the USA
Columbia, SC
22 August 2023

21978246R00063